*International standards and
guiding principles on labour law
and labour relations, 1989*

Labour-Management Relations Series No. 74

# *International standards and guiding principles on labour law and labour relations, 1989*

International Labour Office   Geneva

Copyright © International Labour Organisation 1992
First published 1992

Publications of the International Labour Office enjoy copyright under Protocol 2 of the Universal Copyright Convention. Nevertheless, short excerpts from them may be reproduced without authorisation, on condition that the source is indicated. For rights of reproduction or translation, application should be made to the Publications Branch (Rights and Permissions), International Labour Office, CH-1211 Geneva 22, Switzerland. The International Labour Office welcomes such applications.

---

ILO
*International standards and guiding principles on labour law and labour relations, 1989*
Geneva, International Labour Office, 1992. Labour-Management Relations Series, No. 74
/Text/s, /ILO Convention/s, /ILO Recommendation/s, /ILO Resolution/s, /Labour Relations/.
13.06.1
ISBN 92-2-107097-2
ISSN 0538-8325

Also published in French: *Normes internationales et principes généraux en matière de relations professionnelles, 1989* (ISBN 92-2-207097-6), Geneva, 1991 (Série Relations professionnelles, n° 74); and in Spanish: *Normas internacionales y principios generales en materia de relaciones de trabajo, 1989* (ISBN 92-2-307097-X), Geneva, 1992 (Serie Relaciones de Trabajo, núm. 74)

*ILO Cataloguing in Publication Data*

---

The designations employed in ILO publications, which are in conformity with United Nations practice, and the presentation of material therein do not imply the expression of any opinion whatsoever on the part of the International Labour Office concerning the legal status of any country, area or territory or of its authorities, or concerning the delimitation of its frontiers.

The responsibility for opinions expressed in signed articles, studies and other contributions rests solely with their authors, and publication does not constitute an endorsement by the International Labour Office of the opinions expressed in them.

Reference to names of firms and commercial products and processes does not imply their endorsement by the International Labour Office, and any failure to mention a particular firm, commercial product or process is not a sign of disapproval.

ILO publications can be obtained through major booksellers or ILO local offices in many countries, or direct from ILO Publications, International Labour Office, CH-1211 Geneva 22, Switzerland. A catalogue or list of new publications will be sent free of charge from the above address.

Labour-Management Relations Series No. 74

# *International standards and guiding principles on labour law and labour relations, 1989*

International Labour Office   Geneva

Copyright © International Labour Organisation 1992
First published 1992

Publications of the International Labour Office enjoy copyright under Protocol 2 of the Universal Copyright Convention. Nevertheless, short excerpts from them may be reproduced without authorisation, on condition that the source is indicated. For rights of reproduction or translation, application should be made to the Publications Branch (Rights and Permissions), International Labour Office, CH-1211 Geneva 22, Switzerland. The International Labour Office welcomes such applications.

---

ILO
*International standards and guiding principles on labour law and labour relations, 1989*
Geneva, International Labour Office, 1992. Labour-Management Relations Series, No. 74
/Text/s, /ILO Convention/s, /ILO Recommendation/s, /ILO Resolution/s, /Labour Relations/.
13.06.1
ISBN 92-2-107097-2
ISSN 0538-8325

Also published in French: *Normes internationales et principes généraux en matière de relations professionnelles, 1989* (ISBN 92-2-207097-6), Geneva, 1991 (Série Relations professionnelles, n° 74); and in Spanish: *Normas internacionales y principios generales en materia de relaciones de trabajo, 1989* (ISBN 92-2-307097-X), Geneva, 1992 (Serie Relaciones de Trabajo, núm. 74)

ILO Cataloguing in Publication Data

---

The designations employed in ILO publications, which are in conformity with United Nations practice, and the presentation of material therein do not imply the expression of any opinion whatsoever on the part of the International Labour Office concerning the legal status of any country, area or territory or of its authorities, or concerning the delimitation of its frontiers.
The responsibility for opinions expressed in signed articles, studies and other contributions rests solely with their authors, and publication does not constitute an endorsement by the International Labour Office of the opinions expressed in them.
Reference to names of firms and commercial products and processes does not imply their endorsement by the International Labour Office, and any failure to mention a particular firm, commercial product or process is not a sign of disapproval.

ILO publications can be obtained through major booksellers or ILO local offices in many countries, or direct from ILO Publications, International Labour Office, CH-1211 Geneva 22, Switzerland. A catalogue or list of new publications will be sent free of charge from the above address.

# Preface

This issue of the Labour Management Relations Series consists essentially of an updating of the five preceding issues (namely, Nos. 4, 14, 24, 34 and 44), published in 1959, 1962, 1965, 1969 and 1975 respectively. It is addressed to all those interested in the development of industrial relations in the world today; its objective is to make available to them the texts of the main international standards and the guiding principles adopted by the International Labour Organisation up to 1989, in the fields of freedom of association, collective bargaining, labour disputes settlement, enterprise-level labour relations, labour relations in the public service, tripartism, employment security and remuneration.

The first part of this compilation contains international standards adopted by the International Labour Conference, namely the Declaration of Philadelphia and a series of Conventions and Recommendations grouped by subject. The second part includes other texts also grouped by subject: Resolutions of the International Labour Conference, Conclusions adopted by the Regional Conferences and by the Industrial Committees or other analogous meetings, guidelines adopted by the meeting of Experts on Pay systems, extracts from the Tripartite declaration of Principles Concerning Multinational Enterprises and Social Policy adopted by the Governing Body of the International Labour Office.

Besides Conventions and Recommendations, this issue does not, with certain exceptions, reproduce the documents already published in previous volumes. Readers interested in these documents can find in Annex 1 the list of the texts published in No. 44 of the Labour Management Series and which are not presented in this issue.

Unlike preceding issues, this text does not contain the ILO list of publications of the main reports and articles on labour relations. The list now forms part of a separate publication: *Publications and documents concerning labour law and labour relations*, periodically updated by the Labour Law and Labour Relations Branch.

**Note**

It should be summarily recalled that from a legal point of view, differences exist between various kinds of instruments adopted by the ILO and its bodies.

The international labour Conventions are subject to ratification. Member States which have ratified a Convention are committed to apply the standards contained in the Convention and to submit regularly to the International Labour Office a report concerning the measures taken.

The Recommendations aim at setting standards which would guide member States' decisions at the national level.

The objective of resolutions and conclusions is to indicate to the ILO and the member States the direction to follow with regard to the measures to be taken in the application of standards and principles in specific fields.

# Contents

**Preface** v

## Part I  International instruments adopted by the International Labour Conference

**The Declaration of Philadelphia** 3

**International Labour Conventions and Recommendations** 5

Freedom of association 5
1. Convention No. 11: Right of Association (Agriculture), 1921 5
2. Convention No. 87: Freedom of Association and Protection of the Right to Organise, 1948 5
3. Convention No. 135: Workers' Representatives, 1971 8
4. Recommendation No. 143: Workers' Representatives, 1971 9
5. Convention No. 141: Rural Workers' Organisations, 1975 13
6. Recommendation No. 149: Rural Workers' Organisations, 1975 15

Collective Bargaining 22
1. Convention No. 98: Right to Organise and Collective Bargaining, 1949 22
2. Recommendation No. 91: Collective Agreements, 1951 23
3. Convention No. 154: Collective Bargaining, 1981 25
4. Recommendation No. 163: Collective Bargaining, 1981 28

Labour dispute settlement 31
1. Recommendation No. 92: Voluntary Conciliation and Arbitration, 1951 31

Labour-management relations at the enterprise level 33
1. Recommendation No. 94: Co-operation at the Level of the Undertaking, 1952 33
2. Recommendation No. 129: Communications within the Undertaking, 1967 33
3. Recommendation No. 130: Examination of Grievances, 1967 36

Labour relations in the public service 40
1. Convention No. 151: Labour Relations (Public Service), 1978 40
2. Recommendation No. 159: Labour Relations (Public Service), 1978 40

Tripartism 45
1. Recommendation No. 113: Consultation (Industrial and National Levels), 1960 45
2. Convention No. 144: Tripartite Consultation (International Labour Standards), 1976 46
3. Recommendation No. 152: Tripartite Consultation (Activities of the International Labour Organisation), 1976 48

| | | |
|---|---|---|
| Employment security | | 51 |
| 1. Convention No. 158: Termination of Employment, 1982 | | 51 |
| 2. Recommendation No. 166: Termination of Employment, 1982 | | 56 |
| Remuneration | | 62 |
| 1. Convention No. 26: Minimum Wage-Fixing Machinery, 1928 | | 62 |
| 2. Recommendation No. 30: Minimum Wage-Fixing Machinery, 1928 | | 63 |
| 3. Convention No. 95: Protection of Wages, 1949 | | 66 |
| 4. Recommendation No. 85: Protection of Wages, 1949 | | 70 |
| 5. Convention No. 99: Minimum Wage Fixing Machinery (Agriculture), 1951 | | 72 |
| 6. Recommendation No. 89: Minimum Wage Fixing Machinery in Agriculture, 1951 | | 74 |
| 7. Convention No. 100: Equal Remuneration, 1951 | | 76 |
| 8. Recommendation No. 90: Equal Remuneration, 1951 | | 77 |
| 9. Convention No. 131: Minimum Wage Fixing, 1970 | | 78 |
| 10. Recommendation No. 135: Minimum Wage Fixing, 1970 | | 81 |

**Part II Other instruments**

| | | |
|---|---|---|
| A. | **Resolutions adopted by the International Labour Conference** | 87 |
| | 1. Resolution concerning Trade Union Rights and Their Relation to Civil Liberties, 1970 | 87 |
| | 2. Resolution on Labour and Social Implications of Automation and Other Technological Developments, 1972 | 90 |
| | 3. Resolution concerning the Development of the ILO's Programme for the Improvement of Industrial Relations, 1979 | 98 |
| B. | **Resolution of the Preparatory Technical Maritime Conference** | 101 |
| | 1. Resolution concerning Industrial Relations in the Shipping Industry, 1975 | 101 |
| C. | **Resolutions and Conclusions adopted by the ILO Regional Conferences** | 103 |
| | Freedom of association and labour relations | 103 |
| | 1. Resolution concerning international labour standards in Asia, in particular those relating to human rights and trade union freedoms, 8th Asian Regional Conference, Colombo, 1975 | 103 |
| | 2. Conclusions concerning Freedom of association, labour relations and development in Asia, 9th Asian Regional Conference, Manila, 1980 | 106 |
| | 3. Conclusions concerning labour relations and development in the Americas, 12th Conference of American States Members of the International Labour Organisation, Montreal, 1986 | 110 |
| | Tripartism | 115 |
| | 1. Resolution concerning the strengthening and furthering of tripartite co-operation, 10th Conference of American States Members of the International Labour Organisation, Mexico, 1974 | 115 |
| D. | **Conclusions and other instruments adopted by industrial committees, experts meetings and other technical meetings convened by the ILO Governing Body** | 117 |
| | Labour relations and collective bargaining | 117 |

1. Conclusions concerning collective bargaining problems and practices on plantations and the exercise of trade union rights, Committee on Work on Plantations, 7th Session, 1976 ........................................................................ 117
2. Conclusions concerning industrial relations and collective bargaining practices in the chemical industries, Chemical Industries Committee, 9th Session, 1982 ........................................................................ 120
3. Conclusions concerning collective bargaining as a means of improving the working and living conditions of workers in the metal trades, Metal Trades Committee, 11th Session, 1983 ........................................................................ 123

Labour Relations in the Public Service ........................................................................ 128

1. Conclusions concerning disciplinary codes and procedures in the public service and concerning conditions of work and employment of public service personnel of local, regional or provincial authorities, Joint Committee on the Public Service, 2nd Session, 1976 ........................................................................ 128
2. Conclusions on labour disputes and procedures for their settlement in the public service, Meeting on the Settlement of Labour Disputes in the Public Service, 1986 ........................................................................ 133
3. Conclusions concerning joint consultation, negotiating and collective bargaining rights with regard to determining pay and conditions of employment in the public service, Joint Committee on the Public Service, 4th Session, 1988 ........................................................................ 135

Labour relations in health and medical services ........................................................................ 137

1. Conclusions on employment, labour-management relations, remuneration, ethical problems, working time and occupational health and safety in health and medical services, Joint Meeting on Employment and Conditions of Work in Health and Medical Services, 1985 ........................................................................ 137

Employment security ........................................................................ 140

1. Conclusions concerning social problems of contract, subcontract and casual labour in the petroleum industry, Petroleum Committee, 8th Session, 1973 ........................................................................ 141
2. Conclusions concerning employment security in civil aviation, Tripartite Technical Meeting for Civil Aviation, 1977 ........................................................................ 142
3. Conclusions concerning security of employment and income in the light of structural changes in the textiles industry, Textiles Committee, 11th Session, 1984 ........................................................................ 145

Remuneration ........................................................................ 150

1. Guidelines on the selection, design and administration of appropriate pay systems, Meeting of Experts on Pay Systems, 1983 ........................................................................ 151
2. Conclusions concerning methods of wage determination in the postal and telecommunications sector, Joint Committee for Postal and Telecommunications Services, 1st Session, 1984 ........................................................................ 161

Multinational enterprises ........................................................................ 166

1. Tripartite Declaration of Principles concerning Multinational Enterprises and Social Policy (extract), ILO Governing Body, 204th Session, 1977 ........................................................................ 166

**Annex 1. Documents published in the Labour-Management Relations Series, No. 44, which were not reproduced in the present issue** ........................................................................ 170

**Annex 2. Previous volumes in the Labour-Management Relations Series** ........................................................................ 177

Part I

*International instruments adopted
by the International Labour Conference*

# The Declaration of Philadelphia[1]

## I

The Conference reaffirms the fundamental principles on which the Organisation is based and, in particular, that:
(a) labour is not a commodity;
(b) freedom of expression and of association are essential to sustained progress;
(c) poverty anywhere constitutes a danger to prosperity everywhere;
(d) the war against want requires to be carried on with unrelenting vigour within each nation, and by continuous and concerted international effort in which the representatives of workers and employers, enjoying equal status with those of governments, join with them in free discussion and democratic decision with a view to the promotion of the common welfare.

## II

Believing that experience has fully demonstrated the truth of the statement in the Constitution of the International Labour Organisation that lasting peace can be established only if it is based on social justice, the Conference affirms that:
(a) all human beings, irrespective of race, creed or sex, have the right to pursue both their material well-being and their spiritual development in conditions of freedom and dignity, of economic security and equal opportunity;
(b) the attainment of the conditions in which this shall be possible must constitute the central aim of national and international policy;
(c) all national and international policies and measures, in particular those of an economic and financial character, should be judged in this light and accepted only in so far as they may be held to promote and not to hinder the achievement of this fundamental objective;
(d) it is a responsibility of the International Labour Organisation to examine and consider all international economic and financial policies and measures in the light of this fundamental objective;
(e) in discharging the tasks entrusted to it the International Labour Organisation, having considered all relevant economic and financial factors, may include in its decisions and recommendations any provision which it considers appropriate.

## III

The Conference recognises the solemn obligation of the International Labour Organisation to further among the nations of the world programmes which will achieve:

[1] On 10 May 1944, at the 26th Session of the International Labour Conference held in Philadelphia, the objects set forth in the Preamble to the Constitution of the ILO were reaffirmed in a Declaration concerning the aims and purposes of the ILO. This Declaration has now been integrated as an annex in the ILO Constitution.

*(a)* full employment and the raising of standards of living;

*(b)* the employment of workers in the occupations in which they can have the satisfaction of giving the fullest measure of their skill and attainments and make their greatest contribution to the common well-being;

*(c)* the provision, as a means to the attainment of this end and under adequate guarantees for all concerned, of facilities for training and the transfer of labour, including migration for employment and settlement;

*(d)* policies in regard to wages and earnings, hours and other conditions of work calculated to ensure a just share of the fruits of progress to all, and a minimum living wage to all employed and in need of such protection;

*(e)* the effective recognition of the right of collective bargaining, the co-operation of management and labour in the continuous improvement of productive efficiency, and the collaboration of workers and employers in the preparation and application of social and economic measures;

*(f)* the extension of social security measures to provide a basic income to all in need of such protection and comprehensive medical care;

*(g)* adequate protection for the life and health of workers in all occupations;

*(h)* provision for child welfare and maternity protection;

*(i)* the provision of adequate nutrition, housing and facilities for recreation and culture;

*(j)* the assurance of equality of educational and vocational opportunity.

## IV

Confident that the fuller and broader utilisation of the world's productive resources necessary for the achievement of the objectives set forth in this Declaration can be secured by effective international and national action, including measures to expand production and consumption, to avoid severe economic fluctuations, to promote the economic and social advancement of the less developed regions of the world, to assure greater stability in world prices of primary products, and to promote a high and steady volume of international trade, the Conference pledges the full co-operation of the International Labour Organisation with such international bodies as may be entrusted with a share of the responsibility for this great task and for the promotion of the health, education and well-being of all peoples.

## V

The Conference affirms that the principles set forth in this Declaration are fully applicable to all peoples everywhere and that, while the manner of their application must be determined with due regard to the stage of social and economic development reached by each people, their progressive application to peoples who are still dependent, as well as to those who have already achieved self-government is a matter of concern to the whole civilised world.

# International Labour Conventions and Recommendations

## Freedom of association

### 1. Convention No. 11
### Right of Association (Agriculture), 1921[1]

The General Conference of the International Labour Organisation,

Having been convened at Geneva by the Governing Body of the International Labour Office, and having met in its Third Session on 25 October 1921, and

Having decided upon the adoption of certain proposals with regard to the rights of association and combination of agricultural workers, which is included in the fourth item of the agenda of the Session, and

Having determined that these proposals shall take the form of an international Convention,

adopts the following Convention, which may be cited as the Right of Association (Agriculture) Convention, 1921, for ratification by the Members of the International Labour Organisation in accordance with the provisions of the Constitution of the International Labour Organisation:

*Article 1*

Each Member of the International Labour Organisation which ratifies this Convention undertakes to secure to all those engaged in agriculture the same rights of association and combination as to industrial workers, and to repeal any statutory or other provisions restricting such rights in the case of those engaged in agriculture.

### 2. Convention No. 87
### Freedom of Association and Protection of the Right to Organise, 1948[2]

The General Conference of the International Labour organisation,

Having been convened at San Francisco by the Governing Body of the International Labour Office, and having met in its 31st Session on 17 June 1948,

Having decided to adopt, in the form of a Convention, certain proposals concerning freedom of association and protection of the right to organise, which is the seventh item on the agenda of the session,

---

[1] Date of coming into force: 11 May 1923.
[2] Date of coming into force: 4 July 1950

Considering that the Preamble to the Constitution of the International Labour Organisation declares "recognition of the principle of freedom of association" to be a means of improving conditions of labour and of establishing peace,

Considering that the Declaration of Philadelphia reaffirms that "freedom of expression and of association are essential to sustained progress",

Considering that the International Labour Conference, at its 30th Session, unanimously adopted the principles which should form the basis for international regulation,

Considering that the General Assembly of the United Nations, at its Second Session, endorsed these principles and requested the International Labour Organisation to continue every effort in order that it may be possible to adopt one or several international conventions,

adopts this ninth day of July of the year one thousand nine hundred and forty-eight the following Convention, which may be cited as the Freedom of Association and Protection of the Right to Organise Convention, 1948:

## Part I. Freedom of association

### Article 1

Each Member of the International Labour Organisation for which this Convention is in force undertakes to give effect to the following provisions.

### Article 2

Workers and employers, without distinction whatsoever, shall have the right to establish and, subject only to the rules of the organisation concerned, to join organisations of their own choosing without previous authorisation.

### Article 3

1. Workers' and employers' organisations shall have the right to draw up their constitutions and rules, to elect their representatives in full freedom, to organise their administration and activities and to formulate their programmes.

2. The public authorities shall refrain from any interference which would restrict this right or impede the lawful exercise thereof.

### Article 4

Workers' and employers' organisations shall not be liable to be dissolved or suspended by administrative authority.

## Article 5

Workers' and employers' organisations shall have the right to establish and join federations and confederations and any such organisation, federation or confederation shall have the right to affiliate with international organisations of workers and employers.

## Article 6

The provisions of Articles 2, 3 and 4 hereof apply to federations and confederations of workers' and employers' organisations.

## Article 7

The acquisition of legal personality by workers' and employers' organisations, federations and confederations shall not be made subject to conditions of such a character as to restrict the application of the provisions of Articles 2, 3 and 4 hereof.

## Article 8

1. In exercising the rights provided for in this Convention workers and employers and their respective organisations, like other persons or organised collectivities, shall respect the law of the land.
2. The law of the land shall not be such as to impair, nor shall it be so applied as to impair, the guarantees provided for in this Convention.

## Article 9

1. The extent to which the guarantees provided for in this Convention shall apply to the armed forces and the police shall be determined by national laws or regulations.
2. In accordance with the principles set forth in paragraph 8 of article 19 of the Constitution of the International Labour Organisation the ratification of this Convention by any Member shall not be deemed to affect any existing law, award, custom or agreement in virtue of which members of the armed forces or the police enjoy any right guaranteed by this Convention.

## Article 10

In this Convention the term "organisations" means any organisation of workers or of employers for furthering and defending the interests of workers or of employers.

## Part II. Protection of the right to organise

### Article 11

Each Member of the International Labour Organisation for which this Convention is in force undertakes to take all necessary and appropriate measures to ensure that workers and employers may exercise freely the right to organise.

## 3. Convention No. 135
### Workers' Representatives, 1971[1]

The General Conference of the International Labour Organisation,

Having been convened at Geneva by the Governing Body of the International Labour Office, and having met in its Fifty-sixth Session on 2 June 1971, and

Noting the terms of the Right to Organise and Collective Bargaining Convention, 1949, which provides for protection of workers against acts of anti-union discrimination in respect of their employment, and

Considering that it is desirable to supplement these terms with respect to workers' representatives, and

Having decided upon the adoption of certain proposals with regard to protection and facilities afforded to workers' representatives in the undertaking, which is the fifth item on the agenda of the session, and

Having determined that these proposals shall take the form of an international Convention,

adopts this twenty-third day of June of the year one thousand nine hundred and seventy-one the following Convention, which may be cited as the Workers' Representatives Convention, 1971:

### Article 1

Workers' representatives in the undertaking shall enjoy effective protection against any act prejudicial to them, including dismissal, based on their status or activities as a workers' representative or on union membership or participation in union activities, in so far as they act in conformity with existing laws or collective agreements or other jointly agreed arrangements.

### Article 2

1. Such facilities in the undertaking shall be afforded to workers' representatives as may be appropriate in order to enable them to carry out their functions promptly and efficiently.

2. In this connection account shall be taken of the characteristics of the industrial relations system of the country and the needs, size and capabilities of the undertaking concerned.

---

[1] Date of coming into force: 30 June 1973

3. The granting of such facilities shall not impair the efficient operation of the undertaking concerned.

### Article 3

For the purpose of this Convention the term "workers' representatives" means persons who are recognised as such under national law or practice, whether they are—

*(a)* trade union representatives, namely, representatives designated or elected by trade unions or by the members of such unions; or

*(b)* elected representatives, namely, representatives who are freely elected by the workers of the undertaking in accordance with provisions of national laws or regulations or of collective agreements and whose functions do not include activities which are recognised as the exclusive prerogative of trade unions in the country concerned.

### Article 4

National laws or regulations, collective agreements, arbitration awards or court decisions may determine the type or types of workers' representatives which shall be entitled to the protection and facilities provided for in this Convention.

### Article 5

Where there exist in the same undertaking both trade union representatives and elected representatives, appropriate measures shall be taken, wherever necessary, to ensure that the existence of elected representatives is not used to undermine the position of the trade unions concerned or their representatives and to encourage co-operation on all relevant matters between the elected representatives and the trade unions concerned and their representatives.

### Article 6

Effect may be given to this Convention through national laws or regulations or collective agreements, or in any other manner consistent with national practice.

## 4. *Recommendation No. 143*
*Workers' Representatives, 1971*

The General Conference of the International Labour Organisation,

Having been convened at Geneva by the Governing Body of the International Labour Office, and having met in its Fifty-sixth Session on 2 June 1971, and

Having adopted the Workers' Representatives Convention, 1971, and

Having decided upon the adoption of certain proposals with regard to protection and facilities afforded to workers' representatives in the undertaking, which is the fifth item on the agenda of the session, and

Having determined that these proposals shall take the form of a Recommendation,

adopts this twenty-third day of June of the year one thousand nine hundred and seventy-one the following Recommendation, which may be cited as the Workers' Representatives Recommendation, 1971.

## I. Methods of implementation

1. Effect may be given to this Recommendation through national laws or regulations or collective agreements, or in any other manner consistent with national practice.

## II. General provisions

2. For the purpose of this Recommendation the term "workers' representatives" means persons who are recognised as such under national law or practice, whether they are—

(a) trade union representatives, namely representatives designated or elected by trade unions or by the members of such unions; or

(b) elected representatives, namely representatives who are freely elected by the workers of the undertaking in accordance with provisions of national laws or regulations or of collective agreements and whose functions do not include activities which are recognised as the exclusive prerogative of trade unions in the country concerned.

3. National laws or regulations, collective agreements, arbitration awards or court decisions may determine the type or types of workers' representatives which should be entitled to the protection and facilities provided for in this Recommendation.

4. Where there exist in the same undertaking both trade union representatives and elected representatives, appropriate measures should be taken, wherever necessary, to ensure that the existence of elected representatives is not used to undermine the position of the trade unions concerned or their representatives and to encourage co-operation on all relevant matters between the elected representatives and the trade unions concerned and their representatives.

## III. Protection of workers' representatives

5. Workers' representatives in the undertaking should enjoy effective protection against any act prejudicial to them, including dismissal, based on their status or activities as a workers' representative or on union membership or participation in union activities, in so far as they act in conformity with existing laws or collective agreements or other jointly agreed arrangements.

6. (1) Where there are not sufficient relevant protective measures applicable to workers in general, specific measures should be taken to ensure effective protection of workers' representatives.

(2) These might include such measures as the following:
- (a) detailed and precise definition of the reasons justifying termination of employment of workers' representatives;
- (b) a requirement of consultation with, an advisory opinion from, or agreement of an independent body, public or private, or a joint body, before the dismissal of a workers' representative becomes final;
- (c) a special recourse procedure open to workers' representatives who consider that their employment has been unjustifiably terminated, or that they have been subjected to an unfavourable change in their conditions of employment or to unfair treatment;
- (d) in respect of the unjustified termination of employment of workers' representatives, provision for an effective remedy which, unless this is contrary to basic principles of the law of the country concerned, should include the reinstatement of such representatives in their job, with payment of unpaid wages and with maintenance of their acquired rights;
- (e) provision for laying upon the employer, in the case of any alleged discriminatory dismissal or unfavourable change in the conditions of employment of a workers' representative, the burden of proving that such action was justified;
- (f) recognition of a priority to be given to workers' representatives with regard to their retention in employment in case of reduction of the work force.

7. (1) Protection afforded under Paragraph 5 of this Recommendation should also apply to workers who are candidates, or have been nominated as candidates through such appropriate procedures as may exist, for election or appointment as workers' representatives.

(2) The same protection might also be afforded to workers who have ceased to be workers' representatives.

(3) The period during which such protection is enjoyed by the persons referred to in this Paragraph may be determined by the methods of implementation referred to in Paragraph 1 of this Recommendation.

8. (1) Persons who, upon termination of their mandate as workers' representatives in the undertaking in which they have been employed, resume work in that undertaking should retain, or have restored, all their rights, including those related to the nature of their job, to wages and to seniority.

(2) The questions whether, and to what extent, the provisions of subparagraph (1) of this Paragraph should apply to workers' representatives who have exercised their functions mainly outside the undertaking concerned should be left to national laws or regulations, collective agreements, arbitration awards or court decisions.

## IV. Facilities to be afforded to workers' representatives

9. (1) Such facilities in the undertaking should be afforded to workers' representatives as may be appropriate in order to enable them to carry out their functions promptly and efficiently.

(2) In this connection account should be taken of the characteristics of the industrial relations system of the country and the needs, size and capabilities of the undertaking concerned.

(3) The granting of such facilities should not impair the efficient operation of the undertaking concerned.

10. (1) Workers' representatives in the undertaking should be afforded the necessary time off from work, without loss of pay or social and fringe benefits, for carrying out their representation functions in the undertaking.

(2) In the absence of appropriate provisions, a workers' representative may be required to obtain permission from his immediate supervisor or another appropriate representative of management designated for this purpose before he takes time off from work, such permission not to be unreasonably withheld.

(3) Reasonable limits may be set on the amount of time off which is granted to workers' representatives under subparagraph (1) of this Paragraph.

11. (1) In order to enable them to carry out their functions effectively, workers representatives should be afforded the necessary time off for attending trade union meetings, training courses, seminars, congresses and conferences.

(2) Time off afforded under subparagraph (1) of this Paragraph should be afforded without loss of pay or social and fringe benefits, it being understood that the question of who should bear the resulting costs may be determined by the methods of implementation referred to in paragraph 1 of this Recommendation.

12. Workers' representatives in the undertaking should be granted access to all workplaces in the undertaking, where such access is necessary to enable them to carry out their representation functions.

13. Workers' representatives should be granted without undue delay access to the management of the undertaking and to management representatives empowered to take decisions, as may be necessary for the proper exercise of their functions.

14. In the absence of other arrangements for the collection of trade union dues, workers' representatives authorised to do so by the trade union should be permitted to collect such dues regularly on the premises of the undertaking.

15. (1) Workers' representatives acting on behalf of a trade union should be authorised to post trade union notices on the premises of the undertaking in a place or places agreed on with the management and to which the workers have easy access.

(2) The management should permit workers' representatives acting on behalf of a trade union to distribute news sheets, pamphlets, publications and other documents of the union among the workers of the undertaking.

(3) The union notices and documents referred to in this Paragraph should relate to normal trade union activities and their posting and distribution should not prejudice the orderly operation and tidiness of the undertaking.

(4) Workers' representatives who are elected representatives in the meaning of clause (b) of Paragraph 2 of this Recommendation should be given similar facilities consistent with their functions.

16. The management should make available to workers' representatives, under the conditions and to the extent which may be determined by the methods of

implementation referred to in Paragraph 1 of this Recommendation, such material facilities and information as may be necessary for the exercise of their functions.

17. (1) Trade union representatives who are not employed in the undertaking but whose trade union has members employed therein should be granted access to the undertaking.

(2) The determination of the conditions for such access should be left to the methods of implementation referred to in Paragraphs 1 and 3 of this Recommendation.

## 5. Convention No. 141
### Rural Workers' Organisations, 1975

The General Conference of the International Labour Organisation,

Having been convened at Geneva by the Governing Body of the International Labour Office, and having met in its Sixtieth Session on 4 June 1975, and

Recognising that the importance of rural workers in the world makes it urgent to associate them with economic and social development action if their conditions of work and life are to be permanently and effectively improved, and

Noting that in many countries of the world and particularly in developing countries there is massive under-utilisation of land and labour and that this makes it imperative for rural workers to be given every encouragement to develop free and viable organisations capable of protecting and furthering the interests of their members and ensuring their effective contribution to economic and social development, and

Considering that such organisations can and should contribute to the alleviation of the persistent scarcity of food products in various regions of the world, and

Recognising that land reform is in many developing countries an essential factor in the improvement of the conditions of work and life of rural workers and that organisations of such workers should accordingly co-operate and participate actively in the implementation of such reform, and

Recalling the terms of existing international labour Conventions and Recommendations—in particular the Right of Association (Agriculture) Convention, 1921, the Freedom of Association and Protection of the Right to Organise Convention, 1948, and the Right to Organise and Collective Bargaining Convention, 1949—which affirm the right of all workers, including rural workers, to establish free and independent organisations, and the provisions of numerous international labour Conventions and Recommendations applicable to rural workers which call for the participation, inter alia, of workers' organisations in their implementation, and

Noting the joint concern of the United Nations and the specialised agencies, in particular the International Labour Organisation and the Food and Agriculture Organisation of the United Nations, with land reform and rural development, and

Noting that the following standards have been framed in co-operation with the Food and Agriculture Organisation of the United Nations and that, with a view to avoiding duplication, there will be continuing co-operation with that Organisation and with the United Nations in promoting and securing the application of these standards, and

Having decided upon the adoption of certain proposals with regard to organisations of rural workers and their role in economic and social development, which is the fourth item on the agenda of the session, and

Having determined that these proposals shall take the form of an international Convention,

adopts this twenty-third day of June of the year one thousand nine hundred and seventy-five the following Convention, which may be cited as the Rural Workers' Organisations Convention, 1975:

## Article 1

This Convention applies to all types of organisations of rural workers, including organisations not restricted to but representative of rural workers.

## Article 2

1. For the purposes of this Convention, the term "rural workers" means any person engaged in agriculture, handicrafts or a related occupation in a rural area, whether as a wage earner or, subject to the provisions of paragraph 2 of this Article, as a self-employed person such as a tenant, sharecropper or small owner-occupier.

2. This Convention applies only to those tenants, sharecroppers or small owner-occupiers who derive their main income from agriculture, who work the land themselves, with the help only of their family or with the help of occasional outside labour and who do not—

(a) permanently employ workers; or
(b) employ a substantial number of seasonal workers; or
(c) have any land cultivated by sharecroppers or tenants.

## Article 3

1. All categories of rural workers, whether they are wage earners or self-employed, shall have the right to establish and, subject only to the rules of the organisation concerned, to join organisations of their own choosing without previous authorisation.

2. The principles of freedom of association shall be fully respected; rural workers' organisations shall be independent and voluntary in character and shall remain free from all interference, coercion or repression.

3. The acquisition of legal personality by organisations of rural workers shall not be made subject to conditions of such a character as to restrict the application of the provisions of the preceding paragraphs of this Article.

4. In exercising the rights provided for in this Article rural workers and their respective organisations, like other persons or organised collectivities, shall respect the law of the land.

5. The law of the land shall not be such as to impair, nor shall it be so applied as to impair, the guarantees provided for in this Article.

*Article 4*

It shall be an objective of national policy concerning rural development to facilitate the establishment and growth, on a voluntary basis, of strong and independent organisations of rural workers as an effective means of ensuring the participation of rural workers, without discrimination as defined in the Discrimination (Employment and Occupation) Convention, 1958, in economic and social development and in the benefits resulting therefrom.

*Article 5*

1. In order to enable organisations of rural workers to play their role in economic and social development, each Member which ratifies this Convention shall adopt and carry out a policy of active encouragement to these organisations, particularly with a view to eliminating obstacles to their establishment, their growth and the pursuit of their lawful activities, as well as such legislative and administrative discrimination against rural workers' organisations and their members as may exist.

2. Each member which ratifies this Convention shall ensure that national laws or regulations do not, given the special circumstances of the rural sector, inhibit the establishment and growth of rural workers' organisations.

*Article 6*

Steps shall be taken to promote the widest possible understanding of the need to further the development of rural workers' organisations and of the contribution they can make to improving employment opportunities and general conditions of work and life in rural areas as well as to increasing the national income and achieving a better distribution thereof.

## C. Recommendation No. 149
### Rural Workers' Organisations, 1975

The General Conference of the International Labour Organisation,

Having been convened at Geneva by the Governing Body of the International Labour Office, and having met in its Sixtieth Session on 4 June 1975, and

Recognising that the importance of rural workers in the world makes it urgent to associate them with economic and social development action if their conditions of work and life are to be permanently and effectively improved, and

Noting that in many countries of the world and particularly in developing countries there is massive under-utilisation of land and labour and that this makes it imperative for rural workers to be given every encouragement to develop free and viable organisations capable of protecting and furthering the interests of their members and ensuring their effective contribution to economic and social development, and

Considering that such organisations can and should contribute to the alleviation of the persistent scarcity of food products in various regions of the world, and

Recognising that land reform is in many developing countries an essential factor in the improvement of the conditions of work and life of rural workers and that organisations of such workers should accordingly co-operate and participate actively in the implementation of such reform, and

Recalling the terms of existing international labour Conventions and Recommendations—in particular the Right of Association (Agriculture) Convention, 1921, the Freedom of Association and protection of the Right to Organise Convention, 1948, and the right to Organise and Collective Bargaining Convention, 1949—which affirm the right of all workers, including rural workers, to establish free and independent organisations, and the provisions of numerous international labour Conventions and Recommendations applicable to rural workers which call for the participation, inter alia, of workers' organisations in their implementation, and

Noting the joint concern of the United Nations and the specialised agencies, in particular the International Labour Organisation and the Food and Agriculture Organisation of the United Nations, with land reform and rural development, and

Noting that the following standards have been framed in co-operation with the Food and Agriculture Organisation of the United Nations and that, with a view to avoiding duplication, there will be continuing co-operation with that Organisation and with the United Nations in promoting and securing the application of these standards, and

Having decided upon the adoption of certain proposals with regard to organisations of rural workers and their role in economic and social development, which is the fourth item on the agenda of the session, and

Having determined that these proposals shall take the form of a Recommendation,

adopts this twenty-third day of June of the year one thousand nine hundred and seventy-five the following Recommendation, which may be cited as the Rural Workers' Organisations Recommendation, 1975:

## I. General provisions

1. (1) This Recommendation applies to all types of organisations of rural workers, including organisations not restricted to but representative of rural workers.

(2) The Co-operatives (Developing Countries) Recommendation, 1966, further remains applicable to the organisations of rural workers falling within its scope.

2. (1) For the purposes of this Recommendation, the term "rural workers" means any person engaged in agriculture, handicrafts or a related occupation in a rural area, whether as a wage earner or, subject to the provisions of subparagraph (2) of this Paragraph, as a self-employed person such as a tenant, sharecropper or small owner-occupier.

(2) This Recommendation applies only to those tenants, sharecroppers or small owner-occupiers who derive their main income from agriculture, who work the land themselves, with the help only of their family or with the help of occasional outside labour and who do not—

*(a)* permanently employ workers; or

*(b)* employ a substantial number of seasonal workers; or
*(c)* have any land cultivated by sharecroppers or tenants.

3. All categories of rural workers, whether they are wage earners or self-employed, should have the right to establish and, subject only to the rules of the organisation concerned, to join organisations of their own choosing without previous authorisation.

## *II. Role of organisations of rural workers*

4. It should be an objective of national policy concerning rural development to facilitate the establishment and growth, on a voluntary basis, of strong and independent organisations of rural workers as an effective means of ensuring the participation of rural workers, without discrimination as defined in the Discrimination (Employment and Occupation) Convention, 1958, in economic and social development and in the benefits resulting therefrom.

5. Such organisations should, as appropriate, be able to—
*(a)* represent, further and defend the interests of rural workers, for instance by undertaking negotiations and consultations at all levels on behalf of such workers collectively;
*(b)* represent rural workers in connection with the formulation, implementation and evaluation of programmes of rural development and at all stages and levels of national planning;
*(c)* involve the various categories of rural workers, according to the interests of each, actively and from the outset in the implementation of—
   (i) programmes of agricultural development, including the improvement of techniques of production, storing, processing, transport and marketing;
   (ii) programmes of agrarian reform, land settlement and land development;
   (iii) programmes concerning public works, rural industries and rural crafts;
   (iv) rural development programmes, including those implemented with the collaboration of the United Nations, the International Labour Organisation and other specialised agencies;
   (v) the information and education programmes and other activities referred to in Paragraph 15 of this Recommendation;
*(d)* promote and obtain access of rural workers to services such as credit, supply, marketing and transport as well as to technological services;
*(e)* play an active part in the improvement of general and vocational education and training in rural areas as well as in training for community development, training for co-operative and other activities of rural workers' organisations and training for the management thereof;
*(f)* contribute to the improvement of the conditions of work and life of rural workers, including occupational safety and health;
*(g)* promote the extension of social security and basic social services in such fields as housing, health and recreation.

## III. Means of encouraging the growth of organisations of rural workers

6. In order to enable organisations of rural workers to play their role in economic and social development, member States should adopt and carry out a policy of active encouragement to these organisations, particularly with a view to—

*(a)* eliminating obstacles to their establishment, their growth and the pursuit of their lawful activities, as well as such legislative and administrative discrimination against rural workers' organisations and their members as may exist;

*(b)* extending to rural workers' organisations and their members such facilities for vocational education and training as are available to other workers' organisations and their members; and

*(c)* enabling rural workers' organisations to pursue a policy to ensure that social and economic protection and benefits corresponding to those made available to industrial workers or, as appropriate, workers engaged in other non-industrial occupations are also extended to their members.

7. (1) The principles of freedom of association should be fully respected; rural workers' organisations should be independent and voluntary in character and should remain free from all interference, coercion or repression.

(2) The acquisition of legal personality by organisations of rural workers should not be made subject to conditions of such a character as to restrict the application of the provisions of Paragraph 3 and subparagraph (1) of this Paragraph.

(3) In exercising the rights which they enjoy in pursuance of Paragraph 3 and of this Paragraph rural workers and their respective organisations, like other persons or organised collectivities, should respect the law of the land.

(4) The law of the land should not be such as to impair, nor should it be so applied as to impair, the guarantees provided for in Paragraph 3 and in this Paragraph.

### A. Legislative and administrative measures

8. (1) Member States should ensure that national laws or regulations do not, given the special circumstances of the rural sector, inhibit the establishment and growth of rural workers' organisations.

(2) In particular—

*(a)* the principles of right of association and of collective bargaining, in conformity especially with the Right of Association (Agriculture) Convention, 1921, the Freedom of Association and Protection of the Right to Organise Convention, 1948, and the Right to Organise and Collective Bargaining Convention, 1949, should be made fully effective by the application to the rural sector of general laws or regulations on the subject, or by the adoption of special laws or regulations, full account being taken of the needs of all categories of rural workers;

*(b)* relevant laws and regulations should be fully adapted to the special needs of rural areas; for instance—

(i) requirements regarding minimum membership, minimum levels of education and minimum funds should not be permitted to impede the

development of organisations in rural areas where the population is scattered, ill educated and poor;
(ii) problems which may arise concerning the access of organisations of rural workers to their members should be dealt with in a manner respecting the rights of all concerned and in accordance with the terms of the Freedom of Association and Protection of the Right to Organise Convention, 1948, and the Workers' Representative Convention, 1971;
(iii) there should be effective protection of the rural workers concerned against dismissal and against eviction which are based on their status or activities as leaders or members of rural workers' organisations.

9. There should be adequate machinery, whether in the form of labour inspection or of special services, or in some other form, to ensure the effective implementation of laws and regulations concerning rural workers' organisations and their membership.

10. (1) Where rural workers find it difficult, under existing conditions, to take the initiative in establishing and operating their own organisations, existing organisations should be encouraged to give them, at their request, appropriate guidance and assistance corresponding to their interests.

(2) Where necessary, such assistance could on request be supplemented by advisory services staffed by persons qualified to give legal and technical advice and to run educational courses.

11. Appropriate measures should be taken to ensure that there is effective consultation and dialogue with rural workers' organisations on all matters relating to conditions of work and life in rural areas.

12. (1) In connection with the formulation and, as appropriate, the application of economic and social plans and programmes and any other general measures concerning the economic, social or cultural development of rural areas, rural workers' organisations should be associated with planning procedures and institutions, such as statutory boards and committees, development agencies and economic and social councils.

(2) In particular, appropriate measures should be taken to make possible the effective participation of such organisations in the formulation, implementation and evaluation of agrarian reform programmes.

13. Member States should encourage the establishment of procedures and institutions which foster contacts between rural workers' organisations, employers and their organisations and the competent authorities.

## B. *Public information*

14. Steps should be taken, particularly by the competent authority, to promote—
*(a)* the understanding of those directly concerned, such as central, local and other authorities, rural employers and landlords, of the contribution which can be made by rural workers' organisations to the increase and better distribution of national income, to the increase of productive and remunerative employment opportunities in the rural sector, to the raising of the general level of education

and training of the various categories of rural workers and to the improvement of the general conditions of work and life in rural areas;

(b) the understanding of the general public, including, in particular, that in the non-rural sectors of the economy, of the importance of maintaining a proper balance between the development of rural and urban areas, and of the desirability, as a contribution towards ensuring that balance, of furthering the development of rural workers' organisations.

15. These steps might include—

(a) mass information and education campaigns, especially with a view to giving rural workers full and practical information on their rights, so that they may exercise them as necessary;

(b) radio, television and cinema programmes, and periodic articles in the local and national press, describing the conditions of life and work in rural areas and explaining the aims of rural workers' organisations and the results obtained by their activities;

(c) the organisation, locally, of seminars and meetings with the participation of representatives of the various categories of rural workers, of employers and landlords, of other sectors of the population and of local authorities;

(d) the organisation of visits to rural areas of journalists, representatives of employers and workers in industry or commerce, students of universities and schools accompanied by their teachers, and other representatives of the various sectors of the population;

(e) the preparation of suitable curricula for the various types and levels of schools appropriately reflecting the problems of agricultural production and the life of rural workers.

## C. Education and training

16. In order to ensure a sound growth of rural workers' organisations and the rapid assumption of their full role in economic and social development, steps should be taken, by the competent authority among others, to—

(a) impart to the leaders and members of rural workers' organisations knowledge of—

   (i) national laws and regulations and international standards on questions of direct concern to the activity of the organisations, in particular the right of association;
   (ii) the basic principles of the establishment and operation of organisations of rural workers;
   (iii) questions regarding rural development as part of the economic and social development of the country, including agricultural and handicraft production, storing, processing, transport, marketing and trade;
   (iv) principles and techniques of national planning at different levels;
   (v) training manuals and programmes which are published or established by the United Nations, the International Labour Organisation or other specialised agencies and which are designed for the education and training of rural workers;

(b) improve and foster the education of rural workers in general, technical economic and social fields, so as to make them better able both to develop their organisations and understand their rights and to participate actively in rural development; particular attention should be paid to the training of wholly or partly illiterate workers through literacy programmes linked with the practical expansion of their activities;

(c) promote programmes directed to the role which women can and should play in the rural community, integrated in general programmes of education and training to which women and men should have equal opportunities of access;

(d) provide training designed particularly for educators of rural workers, to enable them, for example, to help in the development of co-operative and other appropriate forms of servicing activities which would enable organisations to respond directly to membership needs while fostering their independence through economic self-reliance;

(e) give support to programmes for the promotion of rural youth in general.

17. (1) As an effective means of providing the training and education referred to in Paragraph 16, programmes of workers' education or adult education, specially adapted to national and local conditions and to the social, economic and cultural needs of the various categories of rural workers, including the special needs of women and young persons, should be formulated and applied.

(2) In view of their special knowledge and experience in these fields, trade union movements and existing organisations which represent rural workers might be closely associated with the formulation and carrying out of such programmes.

## D. Financial and material assistance

18. (1) Where, particularly in the initial stages of development, rural workers' organisations consider that they need financial or material assistance, for instance to help them in carrying out programmes of education and training, and where they seek and obtain such assistance, they should receive it in a manner which fully respects their independence and interests and those of their members. Such assistance should be supplementary to the initiative and efforts of rural workers in financing their own organisations.

(2) The foregoing principles apply in all cases of financial and material assistance, including those in which it is the policy of a member State to render such assistance itself.

## Collective bargaining

### 1. Convention No. 98
### Right to Organise and Collective Bargaining, 1949

The General Conference of the International Labour Organisation,

Having been convened at Geneva by the Governing Body of the International Labour Office, and having met in its 32nd Session on 8 June 1949, and

Having decided upon the adoption of certain proposals concerning the application of the principles of the right to organise and to bargain collectively, which is the fourth item on the agenda of the session, and

Having determined that these proposals shall take the form of an international Convention,

adopts this first day of July of the year one thousand nine hundred and forty-nine the following Convention, which may be cited as the Right to Organise and Collective Bargaining Convention, 1949:

#### Article 1

1. Workers shall enjoy adequate protection against acts of anti-union discrimination in respect of their employment.

2. Such protection shall apply more particularly in respect of acts calculated to:

(a) make the employment of a worker subject to the condition that he shall not join a union or shall relinquish trade union membership;

(b) cause the dismissal of or otherwise prejudice a worker by reason of union membership or because of participation in union activities outside working hours, or with the consent of the employer, within working hours.

#### Article 2

1. Workers' and employers' organisations shall enjoy adequate protection against any acts of interference by each other or each other's agents or members in their establishment, functioning or administration.

2. In particular, acts which are designed to promote the establishment of workers' organisations under the domination of employers or employers' organisations, or to support workers' organisations by financial or other means, with the object of placing such organisations under the control of employers or employers' organisations, shall be deemed to constitute acts of interference within the meaning of this Article.

#### Article 3

Machinery appropriate to national conditions shall be established, where necessary, for the purpose of ensuring respect to the right to organise as defined in the preceding Articles.

*Article 4*

Measures appropriate to national conditions shall be taken, where necessary, to encourage and promote the full development and utilisation of machinery for voluntary negotiation between employers or employers' organisations and workers' organisations, with a view to the regulation of terms and conditions of employment by means of collective agreements.

*Article 5*

1. The extent to which the guarantees provided for in this Convention shall apply to the armed forces and the police shall be determined by national laws or regulations.

2. In accordance with the principle set forth in paragraph 8 of article 19 of the Constitution of the International Labour Organisation the ratification of this Convention by any Member shall not be deemed to affect any existing law, award, custom or agreement in virtue of which members of the armed forces or the police enjoy any right guaranteed by this Convention.

*Article 6*

This Convention does not deal with the position of public servants engaged in the administration of the State, nor shall it be construed as prejudicing their rights or status in any way.

## 2. Recommendation No. 91
## Collective Agreements, 1951

The General Conference of the International Labour Organisation,

Having been convened at Geneva by the Governing Body of the International Labour Office, and having met in its 34th Session on 6 June 1951, and

Having decided upon the adoption of certain proposals with regard to collective agreements, which is included in the fifth item on the agenda of the session, and

Having determined that these proposals shall take the form of a Recommendation designed to be implemented by the parties concerned or by the public authorities as may be appropriate under national conditions,

adopts this twenty-ninth day of June of the year one thousand nine hundred and fifty-one, the following Recommendation, which may be cited as the Collective Agreements Recommendation, 1951:

### I. Collective bargaining machinery

1. (1) Machinery appropriate to the conditions existing in each country should be established, by means of agreement or laws or regulations as may be appropriate under national conditions, to negotiate, conclude, revise and renew

collective agreements, or to be available to assist the parties in the negotiation, conclusion, revision and renewal of collective agreements.

(2) The organisation, methods of operation and functions of such machinery should be determined by agreements between the parties or by national laws or regulations, as may be appropriate under national conditions.

## II. Definition of collective agreements

2. (1) For the purpose of this Recommendation, the term "collective agreements" means all agreements in writing regarding working conditions and terms of employment concluded between an employer, a group of employers or one or more employers' organisations, on the one hand, and one or more representative workers' organisations, or, in the absence of such organisations, the representatives of the workers duly elected and authorised by them in accordance with national laws and regulations, on the other.

(2) Nothing in the present definition should be intrepreted as implying the recognition of any association of workers established, dominated or financed by employers or their representatives.

## III. Effects of collective agreements

3. (1) Collective agreements should bind the signatories thereto and those on whose behalf the agreement is concluded. Employers and workers bound by collective agreement should not be able to include in contracts of employment stipulations contrary to those contained in the collective agreement.

(2) Stipulations in such contracts of employment which are contrary to a collective agreement should be regarded as null and void and automatically replaced by the corresponding stipulations of the collective agreement.

(3) Stipulations in contracts of employment which are more favourable to the workers than those prescribed by a collective agreement should not be regarded as contrary to the collective agreement.

(4) If effective observance of the provisions of collective agreements is secured by the parties thereto, the provisions of the preceding subparagraphs should not be regarded as calling for legislative measures.

4. The stipulations of a collective agreement should apply to all workers of the classes concerned employed in the undertakings covered by the agreement unless the agreement specifically provides to the contrary.

## IV. Extension of collective agreements

5. (1) Where appropriate, having regard to established collective bargaining practice, measures, to be determined by national laws or regulations and suited to the conditions of each country, should be taken to extend the application of all or certain stipulations of a collective agreement to all the employers and workers included within the industrial and territorial scope of the agreement.

(2) National laws or regulations may make the extension of a collective agreement subject to the following, among other, conditions:

(a) that the collective agreement already covers a number of the employers and workers concerned which is, in the opinion of the competent authority, sufficiently representative;

(b) that, as a general rule, the request for extension of the agreement shall be made by one or more organisations of workers or employers who are parties to the agreement;

(c) that, prior to the extension of the agreement, the employers and workers to whom the agreement would be made applicable by its extension should be given an opportunity to submit their observations.

## V. Interpretation of collective agreements

6. Disputes arising out of the interpretation of a collective agreement should be submitted to an appropriate procedure for settlement established either by agreement between the parties or by laws or regulations as may be appropriate under national conditions.

## VI. Supervision of application of collective agreements

7. The supervision of the application of collective agreements should be ensured by the employers' and workers' organisations parties to such agreements or by the bodies existing in each country for this purpose or by bodies established ad hoc.

## VII. Miscellaneous

8. National laws and regulations may, among other things, make provision for:

(a) requiring employers bound by collective agreements to take appropriate steps to bring to the notice of the workers concerned the texts of the collective agreements applicable to their undertakings;

(b) the registration or deposit of collective agreements and any subsequent changes made therein;

(c) a minimum period during which, in the absence of any provision to the contrary in the agreement, collective agreements shall be deemed to be binding unless revised or rescinded at an earlier date by the parties.

3. **Convention No. 154**
   **Collective bargaining, 1981**

The General Conference of the International Labour Organisation,

Having been convened at Geneva by the Governing Body of the International Labour Office, and having met in its Sixty-seventh Session on 3 June 1981, and

Reaffirming the provision of the Declaration of Philadelphia recognising "the solemn obligation of the International Labour Organisation to further among the nations of the world programmes which will achieve... the effective recognition of the right of collective bargaining", and noting that this principle is "fully applicable to all people everywhere", and

Having regard to the key importance of existing international standards contained in the Freedom of Association and Protection of the Right to Organise Convention, 1948, the Right to Organise and Collective Bargaining Convention, 1949, the Collective Agreements Recommendation, 1951, the Voluntary Conciliation and Arbitration Recommendation, 1951, the Labour Relations (Public Service) Convention and Recommendation, 1978, and the Labour Administration Convention and Recommendation, 1978, and

Considering that it is desirable to make greater efforts to achieve the objectives of these standards and, particularly, the general principles set out in Article 4 of the Right to Organise and Collective Bargaining Convention, 1949, and in Paragraph 1 of the Collective Agreements Recommendation, 1951, and

Considering accordingly that these standards should be complemented by appropriate measures based on them and aimed at promoting free and voluntary collective bargaining, and

Having decided upon the adoption of certain proposals with regard to the promotion of collective bargaining, which is the fourth item on the agenda of the session, and

Having determined that these proposals shall take the form of an international Convention,

adopts this nineteenth day of June of the year one thousand nine hundred and eighty-one the following Convention, which may be cited as the Collective Bargaining Convention, 1981:

## Part I. Scope and definitions

### Article 1

1. This Convention applies to all branches of economic activity.

2. The extent to which the guarantees provided for in this Convention apply to the armed forces and the police may be determined by national laws or regulations or national practice.

3. As regards the public service, special modalities of application of this Convention may be fixed by national laws or regulations or national practice.

### Article 2

For the purpose of this Convention the term "collective bargaining" extends to all negotiations which take place between an employer, a group of employers or one or more employers' organisations, on the one hand, and one or more workers' organisations, on the other, for—

*(a)* determining working conditions and terms of employment; and/or

*(b)* regulating relations between employers and workers; and/or
*(c)* regulating relations between employers or their organisations and a workers' organisation or workers' organisations.

### Article 3

1. Where national law or practice recognises the existence of workers' representatives as defined in Article 3, subparagraph *(b)*, of the Workers' Representatives Convention, 1971, national law or practice may determine the extent to which the term "collective bargaining" shall also extend, for the purpose of this Convention, to negotiations with these representatives.

2. Where, in pursuance of paragraph 1 of this Article, the term "collective bargaining" also includes negotiations with the workers' representatives referred to in that paragraph, appropriate measures shall be taken, wherever necessary, to ensure that the existence of these representatives is not used to undermine the position of the workers' organisations concerned.

## Part II. Methods of application

### Article 4

The provisions of this Convention shall, in so far as they are not otherwise made effective by means of collective agreements, arbitration awards or in such other manner as may be consistent with national practice, be given effect by national laws or regulations.

## Part III. Promotion of collective bargaining

### Article 5

1. Measures adapted to national conditions shall be taken to promote collective bargaining.

2. The aims of the measures referred to in paragraph 1 of this Article shall be the following:
*(a)* collective bargaining should be made possible for all employers and all groups of workers in the branches of activity covered by this Convention;
*(b)* collective bargaining should be progressively extended to all matters covered by subparagraphs *(a)*, *(b)* and *(c)* of Article 2 of this Convention;
*(c)* the establishment of rules of procedure agreed between employers' and workers' organisations should be encouraged;
*(d)* collective bargaining should not be hampered by the absence of rules governing the procedure to be used or by the inadequacy or inappropriateness of such rules;
*(e)* bodies and procedures for the settlement of labour disputes should be so conceived as to contribute to the promotion of collective bargaining.

*Article 6*

The provisions of this Convention do not preclude the operation of industrial relations systems in which collective bargaining takes place within the framework of conciliation and/or arbitration machinery or institutions, in which machinery or institutions the parties to the collective bargaining process voluntarily participate.

*Article 7*

Measures taken by public authorities to encourage and promote the development of collective bargaining shall be the subject of prior consultation and, whenever possible, agreement between public authorities and employers' and workers' organisations.

*Article 8*

The measures taken with a view to promoting collective bargaining shall not be so conceived or applied as to hamper the freedom of collective bargaining.

## Part IV. Final provisions

*Article 9*

This Convention does not revise any existing Convention or Recommendation.

## 4. Recommendation No. 163
## Collective bargaining, 1981

The General Conference of the International Labour Organisation,

Having been convened at Geneva by the Governing Body of the International Labour Office, and having met in its Sixty-seventh Session on 3 June 1981, and

Having decided upon the adoption of certain proposals with regard to the promotion of collective bargaining, which is the fourth item on the agenda of the session, and

Having determined that these proposals shall take the form of a Recommendation supplementing the Collective Bargaining Convention, 1981,

adopts this nineteenth day of June of the year one thousand nine hundred and eighty-one the following Recommendation, which may be cited as the Collective Bargaining Recommendation, 1981:

### I. Methods of application

1. The provisions of this Recommendation may be applied by national laws or regulations, collective agreements, arbitration awards or in any other manner consistent with national practice.

## II. Means of promoting collective bargaining

2. In so far as necessary, measures adapted to national conditions should be taken to facilitate the establishment and growth, on a voluntary basis, of free, independent and representative employers' and workers' organisations.

3. As appropriate and necessary, measures adapted to national conditions should be taken so that—

(a) representative employers' and workers' organisations are recognised for the purposes of collective bargaining;

(b) in countries in which the competent authorities apply procedures for recognition with a view to determining the organisations to be granted the right to bargain collectively, such determination is based on pre-established and objective criteria with regard to the organisations' representative character, established in consultation with representative employers' and workers' organisations.

4. (1) Measures adapted to national conditions should be taken, if necessary, so that collective bargaining is possible at any level whatsoever, including that of the establishment, the undertaking, the branch of activity, the industry, or the regional or national levels.

(2) In countries where collective bargaining takes place at several levels, the parties to negotiations should seek to ensure that there is co-ordination among these levels.

5. (1) Measures should be taken by the parties to collective bargaining so that their negotiators, at all levels, have the opportunity to obtain appropriate training.

(2) Public authorities may provide assistance to workers' and employers' organisations, at their request, for such training.

(3) The content and supervision of the programmes of such training should be determined by the appropriate workers' or employers' organisations concerned.

(4) Such training should be without prejudice to the right of workers' and employers' organisations to choose their own representatives for the purpose of collective bargaining.

6. Parties to collective bargaining should provide their respective negotiators with the necessary mandate to conduct and conclude negotiations, subject to any provisions for consultations within their respective organisations.

7. (1) Measures adapted to national conditions should be taken, if necessary, so that the parties have access to the information required for meaningful negotiations.

(2) For this purpose—

(a) public and private employers should, at the request of workers' organisations, make available such information on the economic and social situation of the negotiating unit and the undertaking as a whole, as is necessary for meaningful negotiations; where the disclosure of some of this information could be prejudicial to the undertaking, its communication may be made conditional upon a commitment that it would be regarded as confidential to the extent required; the information to be made available may be agreed upon between the parties to collective bargaining;

*(b)* the public authorities should make available such information as is necessary on the over-all economic and social situation of the country and the branch of activity concerned, to the extent to which the disclosure of this information is not prejudicial to the national interest.

8. Measures adapted to national conditions should be taken, if necessary, so that the procedures for the settlement of labour disputes assist the parties to find a solution to the dispute themselves, whether the dispute is one which arose during the negotiation of agreements, one which arose in connection with the interpretation and application of agreements or one covered by the Examination of Grievances Recommendation, 1967.

## III. Final provision

9. This Recommendation does not revise any existing Recommendation.

# Labour dispute settlement

## 1. Recommendation No. 92
### Voluntary Conciliation and Arbitration, 1951

The General Conference of the International Labour Organisation,

Having been convened at Geneva by the Governing Body of the International Labour Office, and having met in its 34th Session on 6 June 1951, and

Having decided upon the adoption of certain proposals with regard to voluntary conciliation and arbitration, which is included in the fifth item on the agenda of the session, and

Having determined that these proposals shall take the form of a Recommendation designed to be implemented by the parties concerned or by the public authorities as may be appropriate under national conditions,

adopts this twenty-ninth day of June of the year one thousand nine hundred and fifty-one the following Recommendation, which may be cited as the Voluntary Conciliation and Arbitration Recommendation, 1951.

### I. Voluntary conciliation

1. Voluntary Conciliation machinery, appropriate to national conditions, should be made available to assist in the prevention and settlement of industrial disputes between employers and workers.

2. Where voluntary conciliation machinery is constituted on a joint basis, it should include equal representation of employers and workers.

3. (1) The procedure should be free of charge and expeditious; such time limits for the proceedings as may be prescribed by national laws or regulations should be fixed in advance and kept to a minimum.

(2) Provision should be made to enable the procedure to be set in motion, either on the initiative of any of the parties to the dispute or ex officio by the voluntary conciliation authority.

4. If a dispute has been submitted to conciliation procedure with the consent of all the parties concerned, the latter should be encouraged to abstain from strikes and lockouts while conciliation is in progress.

5. All agreements which the parties may reach during conciliation procedure or as a result thereof should be drawn up in writing and be regarded as equivalent to agreements concluded in the usual manner.

### II. Voluntary arbitration

6. If a dispute has been submitted to arbitration for final settlement with the consent of all parties concerned, the latter should be encouraged to abstain from strikes and lockouts while the arbitration is in progress and to accept the arbitration award.

## III. General

7. No provision of this Recommendation may be interpreted as limiting, in any way whatsoever, the right to strike.

## Labour-management relations at the enterprise level

### 1. Recommendation No. 94
### Co-operation at the Level of the Undertaking, 1952

The General Conference of the International Labour Organisation,

Having been convened at Geneva by the Governing Body of the International Labour Office, and having met in its 35th Session on 4 June 1952, and

Having decided upon the adoption of certain proposals with regard to consultation and co-operation between employers and workers at the level of the undertaking, which is included in the sixth item on the agenda of the session, and

Having determined that these proposals shall take the form of a Recommendation designed to be implemented by the parties concerned or by the public authorities as may be appropriate under national conditions,

adopts this twenty-sixth day of June of the year one thousand nine hundred and fifty-two the following Recommendation, which may be cited as the Co-operation at the Level of the Undertaking Recommendation, 1952:

1. Appropriate steps should be taken to promote consultation and co-operation between employers and workers at the level of the undertaking on matters of mutual concern not within the scope of collective bargaining machinery, or not normally dealt with by other machinery concerned with the determination of terms and conditions of employment.

2. In accordance with national custom or practice, such consultation and co-operation should be:

(a) facilitated by the encouragement of voluntary agreements between the parties, or

(b) promoted by laws or regulations which would establish bodies for consultation and co-operation and determine their scope, functions, structure and methods of operation as may be appropriate to the conditions in the various undertakings, or

(c) facilitated or promoted by a combination of these methods.

### 2. Recommendation No. 129
### Communications within the Undertaking, 1967

Having been convened at Geneva by the Governing Body of the International Labour Office, and having met in its 51st Session on 7 June 1967, and

Noting the terms of the Co-operation at the Level of the Undertaking Recommendation, 1952, and

Considering that additional standards are called for, and

Having decided upon the adoption of certain proposals with regard to communications within the undertaking, which is included in the fifth item on the agenda of the session, and

Having determined that these proposals shall take the form of a Recommendation, adopts this twenty-eighth day of June of the year one thousand nine hundred and sixty-seven the following Recommendation, which may be cited as the Communications within the Undertaking Recommendation, 1967:

## I. General considerations

1. Each Member should take appropriate action to bring the provisions of this Recommendation to the attention of persons, organisations and authorities who may be concerned with the establishment and application of policies concerning communications between management and workers within undertakings.

2. (1) Employers and their organisations as well as workers and their organisations should, in their common interest, recognise the importance of a climate of mutual understanding and confidence within undertakings that is favourable both to the efficiency of the undertaking and to the aspirations of the workers.

(2) This climate should be promoted by the rapid dissemination and exchange of information, as complete and objective as possible, relating to the various aspects of the life of the undertaking and to the social conditions of the workers.

(3) With a view to the development of such a climate management should, after consultation with workers' representatives, adopt appropriate measures to apply an effective policy of communication with the workers and their representatives.

3. An effective policy of communication should ensure that information is given and that consultation takes place between the parties concerned before decisions on matters of major interest are taken by management, in so far as disclosure of the information will not cause damage to either party.

4. The communication methods should in no way derogate from freedom of association; they should in no way cause prejudice to freely chosen workers' representatives or to their organisations or curtail the functions of bodies representative of the workers in conformity with national law and practice.

5. Employers' and workers' organisations should have mutual consultations and exchanges of views in order to examine the measures to be taken with a view to encouraging and promoting the acceptance of communications policies and their effective application.

6. Steps should be taken to train those concerned in the use of communications methods and to make them, as far as possible, conversant with all the subjects in respect of which communication should take place.

7. In the establishment and application of a communications policy, management, employers' and workers' organisations, bodies representative of the workers and, where appropriate under national conditions, public authorities should be guided by the provisions of Part II below.

## II. Elements for a communications policy within the undertaking

8. Any communications policy should be adapted to the nature of the undertaking concerned, account being taken of its size and of the composition and interests of the work force.

9. With a view to fulfilling its purpose, any communications system within the undertaking should be designed to ensure genuine and regular two-way communication—

(a) between representatives of management (head of the undertaking, department chief, foreman, etc.) and the workers; and

(b) between the head of the undertaking, the director of personnel or any other representative of top management and trade union representatives or such other persons as may, under national law or practice, or under collective agreements, have the task of representing the interests of the workers at the level of the undertaking.

10. Where the management desires to transmit information through workers' representatives, the latter, if they agree to do so, should be given the means to communicate such information rapidly and completely to the workers concerned.

11. Management should, in choosing the channel or channels of communication which it considers appropriate for the type of information to be transmitted, take due account of the difference in the nature of the functions of supervisors and workers' representatives so as not to weaken their respective positions.

12. The selection of the appropriate medium of communication, and its timing, should be on the basis of the circumstances of each particular situation, account being taken of national practice.

13. Media of communication may include—

(a) meetings for the purpose of exchanging views and information;

(b) media aimed at given groups of workers, such as supervisors' bulletins and personnel policy manuals;

(c) mass media such as house journals and magazines; newsletters and information and induction leaflets; notice-boards; annual or financial reports presented in a form understandable to all the workers; employee letters; exhibitions; plant visits; films; filmstrips and slides; radio and television;

(d) media aimed at permitting workers to submit suggestions and to express their ideas on questions relating to the operation of the undertaking.

14. The information to be communicated and its presentation should be determined with a view to mutual understanding in regard to the problems posed by the complexity of the undertaking's activities.

15. (1) The information to be given by management should, account being taken of its nature, be addressed either to the workers' representatives or to the workers and should, as far as possible, include all matters of interest to the workers relating to the operation and future prospects of the undertaking and to the present and future situation of the workers, in so far as disclosure of the information will not cause damage to the parties.

(2) In particular, management should give information regarding—

(a) general conditions of employment, including engagement, transfer and termination of employment;

(b) job descriptions and the place of particular jobs within the structure of the undertaking;

(c) possibilities of training and prospects of advancement within the undertaking;

*(d)* general working conditions;
*(e)* occupational safety and health regulations and instruction for the prevention of accidents and occupational diseases;
*(f)* procedures for the examination of grievances as well as the rules and practices governing their operation and the conditions for having recourse to them;
*(g)* personnel welfare services (medical care, health, canteens, housing, leisure, savings and banking facilities, etc.);
*(h)* social security or social assistance schemes in the undertaking;
*(i)* the regulations of national social security schemes to which the workers are subject by virtue of their employment in the undertaking;
*(j)* the general situation of the undertaking and prospects or plans for its future development;
*(k)* the explanation of decisions which are likely to affect directly or indirectly the situation of workers in the undertaking;
*(l)* methods of consultation and discussion and of co-operation between management and its representatives on the one hand and the workers and their representatives on the other.

(3) In the case of a question which has been the subject of negotiations between the employer and the workers or their representatives in the undertaking or of a collective agreement concluded at a level beyond that of the undertaking, the information should make express reference thereto.

## 3. Recommendation No. 130
## Examination of Grievances, 1967

The General Conference of the International Labour Organisation,

Having been convened at Geneva by the Governing Body of the International Labour Office, and having met in its 51st Session on 7 June 1967, and

Noting the terms of existing international labour Recommendations dealing with various aspects of labour-management relations, and in particular the Collective Agreements Recommendation, 1951, the Voluntary Conciliation and Arbitration Recommendation, 1951, the Co-operation at the Level of the Undertaking Recommendation, 1952, and the Termination of Employment Recommendation, 1963, and

Considering that additional standards are called for, and

Noting the terms of the Communications within the Undertaking Recommendation, 1967, and

Having decided upon the adoption of certain proposals with regard to the examination of grievances within the undertaking, which is included in the fifth item on the agenda of the session, and

Having determined that these proposals shall take the form of a Recommendation,

adopts this twenty-ninth day of June of the year one thousand nine hundred and sixty-seven the following Recommendation, which may be cited as the Examination of Grievances Recommendation, 1967:

## I. Methods of implementation

1. Effect may be given to this Recommendation through national laws or regulations, collective agreements, works rules, or arbitration awards, or in such other manner consistent with national practice as may be appropriate under national conditions.

## II. General principles

2. Any worker who, acting individually or jointly with other workers, considers that he has grounds for a grievance should have the right—
 (a) to submit such grievance without suffering any prejudice whatsoever as a result; and
 (b) to have such grievance examined pursuant to an appropriate procedure.

3. The grounds for a grievance may be any measure or situation which concerns the relations between employer and worker or which affects or may affect the conditions of employment of one or several workers in the undertaking when that measure or situation appears contrary to provisions of an applicable collective agreement or of an individual contract of employment, to works rules, to laws or regulations or to the custom or usage of the occupation, branch of economic activity or country, regard being had to principles of good faith.

4. (1) The provisions of this Recommendation are not applicable to collective claims aimed at the modification of terms and conditions of employment.

 (2) The determination of the distinction between cases in which a complaint submitted by one or more workers is a grievance to be examined under the procedures provided for in this Recommendation and cases in which a complaint is a general claim to be dealt with by means of collective bargaining or under some other procedure for settlement of disputes is a matter for national law or practice.

5. When procedures for the examination of grievances are established through collective agreements, the parties to such an agreement should be encouraged to include therein a provision to the effect that, during the period of its validity, they undertake to promote settlement of grievances under the procedures provided and to abstain from any action which might impede the effective functioning of these procedures.

6. Workers' organisations or the representatives of the workers in the undertaking should be associated, with equal rights and responsibilities, with the employers or their organisations, preferably by way of agreement, in the establishment and implementation of grievance procedures within the undertaking, in conformity with national law or practice.

7. (1) With a view to minimising the number of grievances, the greatest attention should be given to the establishment and proper functioning of a sound personnel policy, which should take into account and respect the rights and interests of the workers.

 (2) In order to achieve such a policy and to solve social questions affecting the workers within the undertaking, management should, before taking a decision, co-operate with the workers' representatives.

8. As far as possible, grievances should be settled within the undertaking itself according to effective procedures which are adapted to the conditions of the country, branch of economic activity and undertaking concerned and which give the parties concerned every assurance of objectivity.

9. None of the provisions of this Recommendation should result in limiting the right of a worker to apply directly to the competent labour authority or to a labour court or other judicial authority in respect of a grievance, where such right is recognised under national laws or regulations.

## III. Procedures within the undertaking

10. (1) As a general rule an attempt should initially be made to settle grievances directly between the worker affected whether assisted or not, and his immediate supervisor.

(2) Where such an attempt at settlement has failed or where the grievance is of such a nature that a direct discussion between the worker affected and his immediate supervisor would be inappropriate, the worker should be entitled to have his case considered at one or more higher steps, depending on the nature of the grievance and on the structure and size of the undertaking.

11. Grievance procedures should be so formulated and applied that there is a real possibility of achieving at each step provided for by the procedure a settlement of the case freely accepted by the worker and the employer.

12. Grievance procedures should be as uncomplicated and as rapid as possible, and appropriate time limits may be prescribed if necessary for this purpose; formality in the application of these procedures should be kept to a minimum.

13. (1) The worker concerned should have the right to participate directly in the grievance procedure and to be assisted or represented during the examination of his grievance by a representative of a workers' organisation, by a representative of the workers in the undertaking, or by any other person of his own choosing, in conformity with national law or practice.

(2) The employer should have the right to be assisted or represented by an employers' organisation.

(3) Any person employed in the same undertaking who assists or represents the worker during the examination of his grievance should, on condition that he acts in conformity with the grievance procedure, enjoy the same protection as that enjoyed by the worker under Paragraph 2, clause (a), of this Recommendation.

14. The worker concerned, or his representative if the latter is employed in the same undertaking, should be allowed sufficient time to participate in the procedure for the examination of the grievance and should not suffer any loss of remuneration because of his absence from work as a result of such participation, account being taken of any rules and practices, including safeguards against abuses, which might be provided for by legislation, collective agreements or other appropriate means.

15. If the parties consider it necessary, minutes of the proceedings may be drawn up in mutual agreement and be available to the parties.

16. (1) Appropriate measures should be taken to ensure that grievance procedures, as well as the rules and practices governing their operation and the conditions for having recourse to them are brought to the knowledge of the workers.

(2) Any worker who has submitted a grievance should be kept informed of the steps being taken under the procedure and of the action taken on his grievance.

## IV. Adjustment of unsettled grievances

17. Where all efforts to settle the grievance within the undertaking have failed, there should be a possibility, account being taken of the nature of the grievance, for final settlement of such grievance through one or more of the following procedures:
 (a) procedures provided for by collective agreement, such as joint examination of the case by employers' and workers' organisations concerned or voluntary arbitration by a person or persons designated with the agreement of the employer and worker concerned or their respective organisations;
 (b) conciliation or arbitration by the competent public authorities;
 (c) recourse to a labour court or other judicial authority;
 (d) any other procedure which may be appropriate under national conditions.

18. (1) The worker should be allowed the time off necessary to take part in the procedures referred to in Paragraph 17 of this Recommendation

(2) Recourse by the worker to any of the procedures provided for in Paragraph 17 should not involve for him any loss of remuneration when his grievance is proved justified in the course of these procedures. Every effort should be made, where possible, for the operation of these procedures outside the working hours of the workers concerned.

## Labour relations in the public service

### 1. Convention 151
### Labour Relations (Public Service),1978

The General Conference of the International Labour Organisation,

Having been convened at Geneva by the Governing Body of the International Labour Office, and having met in its Sixty-fourth Session on 7 June 1978, and

Noting the terms of the Freedom of Association and Protection of the Right to Organise Convention, 1948, the Right to Organise and Collective Bargaining Convention, 1949, and the Workers' Representatives Convention and Recommendation, 1971, and

Recalling that the Right to Organise and Collective Bargaining Convention, 1949, does not cover certain categories of public employees and that the Workers' Representatives Convention and Recommendation, 1971, apply to workers' representatives in the undertaking, and

Noting the considerable expansion of public-service activities in many countries and the need for sound labour relations between public authorities and public employees' organisations, and

Having regard to the great diversity of political, social and economic systems among member States and the differences in practice among them (e.g. as to the respective functions of central and local government, of federal, state and provincial authorities, and of state-owned undertakings and various types of autonomous or semi-autonomous public bodies, as well as to the nature of employment relationships), and

Taking into account the particular problems arising as to the scope of, and definitions for the purpose of, any international instrument, owing to the differences in many countries between private and public employment, as well as the difficulties of interpretation which have arisen in respect of the application of relevant provisions of the Right to Organise and Collective Bargaining Convention, 1949, to public servants, and the observations of the supervisory bodies of the ILO on a number of occasions that some governments have applied these provisions in a manner which excludes large groups of public employees from coverage by that Convention, and

Having decided upon the adoption of certain proposals with regard to freedom of association and procedures for determining conditions of employment in the public service, which is the fifth item on the agenda of the session, and

Having determined that these proposals shall take the form of an international Convention,

adopts this twenty-seventh day of June of the year one thousand nine hundred and seventy-eight the following Convention, which may be cited as the Labour Relations (Public Service) Convention, 1978:

## Part I. Scope and definitions

### Article 1

1. This Convention applies to all persons employed by public authorities, to the extent that more favourable provisions in other international labour Conventions are not applicable to them.

2. The extent to which the guarantees provided for in this Convention shall apply to high-level employees whose functions are normally considered as policy-making or managerial, or to employees whose duties are of a highly confidential nature, shall be determined by national laws or regulations.

3. The extent to which the guarantees provided for in this Convention shall apply to the armed forces and the police shall be determined by national laws or regulations.

### Article 2

For the purpose of this Convention, the term "public employee" means any person covered by the Convention in accordance with Article 1 thereof.

### Article 3

For the purpose of this Convention, the term "public employees' organisation" means any organisation, however composed, the purpose of which is to further and defend the interests of public employees.

## Part II. Protection of the right to organise

### Article 4

1. Public employees shall enjoy adequate protection against acts of anti-union discrimination in respect of their employment.

2. Such protection shall apply more particularly in respect of acts calculated to—
(a) make the employment of public employees subject to the condition that they shall not join or shall relinquish membership of a public employees' organisation;
(b) cause the dismissal of or otherwise prejudice a public employee by reason of membership of a public employees' organisation or because of participation in the normal activities of such an organisation.

### Article 5

1. Public employees' organisations shall enjoy complete independence from public authorities.

2. Public employees' organisations shall enjoy adequate protection against any acts of interference by a public authority in their establishment, functioning or administration.

3. In particular, acts which are designed to promote the establishment of public employees' organisations under the domination of a public authority, or to support public employees' organisations by financial or other means, with the object of placing such organisations under the control of a public authority, shall be deemed to constitute acts of interference within the meaning of this Article.

## Part III. Facilities to be afforded to public employees' organisations

### Article 6

1. Such facilities shall be afforded to the representatives of recognised public employees' organisations as may be appropriate in order to enable them to carry out their functions promptly and efficiently, both during and outside their hours of work.

2. The granting of such facilities shall not impair the efficient operation of the administration or service concerned.

3. The nature and scope of these facilities shall be determined in accordance with the methods referred to in Article 7 of this Convention, or by other appropriate means.

## Part IV. Procedures for determining terms and conditions of employment

### Article 7

Measures appropriate to national conditions shall be taken, where necessary, to encourage and promote the full development and utilisation of machinery for negotiation of terms and conditions of employment between the public authorities concerned and public employees' organisations, or of such other methods as will allow representatives of public employees to participate in the determination of these matters.

## Part V. Settlement of disputes

### Article 8

The settlement of disputes arising in connection with the determination of terms and conditions of employment shall be sought, as may be appropriate to national conditions, through negotiation between the parties or through independent and impartial machinery, such as mediation, conciliation and arbitration, established in such a manner as to ensure the confidence of the parties involved.

## Part VI. Civil and political rights

### Article 9

Public employees shall have, as other workers, the civil and political rights which are essential for the normal exercise of freedom of association, subject only to the obligations arising from their status and the nature of their functions.

## 2. Recommendation No.159
## Labour Relations (Public Service),1978

The General Conference of the International Labour Organisation,

Having been convened at Geneva by the Governing Body of the International Labour Office, and having met in its Sixty-fourth Session on 7 June 1978, and

Having decided upon the adoption of certain proposals with regard to freedom of association and procedures for determining conditions of employment in the public service, which is the fifth item on the agenda of the session, and

Having determined that these proposals shall take the form of a Recommendation supplementing the Labour Relations (Public Service) Convention, 1978,

adopts this twenty-seventh day of June of the year one thousand nine hundred and seventy-eight the following Recommendation, which may be cited as the Labour Relations (Public Service) Recommendation, 1978:

(1) In countries in which procedures for recognition of public employees' organisations apply with a view to determining the organisations to be granted, on a preferential or exclusive basis, the rights provided for under Parts III, IV or V of the Labour Relations (Public Service) Convention, 1978, such determination should be based on objective and pre-established criteria with regard to the organisations' representative character.

(2) The procedures referred to in subparagraph (1) of this Paragraph should be such as not to encourage the proliferation of organisations covering the same categories of employees.

2. (1) In the case of negotiation of terms and conditions of employment in accordance with Part IV of the Labour Relations (Public Service) Convention, 1978, the persons or bodies competent to negotiate on behalf of the public authority concerned and the procedure for giving effect to the agreed terms and conditions of employment should be determined by national laws or regulations or other appropriate means.

(2) Where methods other than negotiation are followed to allow representatives of public employees to participate in the determination of terms and conditions of employment, the procedure for such participation and for final determination of these matters should be determined by national laws or regulations or other appropriate means.

3. Where an agreement is concluded between a public authority and a public employees' organisation in pursuance of Paragraph 2, subparagraph (1), of this Recommendation, the period during which it is to operate and/or the procedure whereby it may be terminated, renewed or revised should normally be specified.

4. In determining the nature and scope of the facilities which should be afforded to representatives of public employees' organisations in accordance with Article 6, Paragraph 3, of the Labour Relations (Public Service) Convention, 1978, regard should be had to the Workers' Representatives Recommendation, 1971.

## Tripartism

### 1. Recommendation No. 113
### Consultation (Industrial and National Levels), 1960

The General conference of the International Labour Organisation,

Having been convened at Geneva by the Governing Body of the International Labour Office, and having met in its 44th Session on 1 June 1960, and

Having decided upon the adoption of certain proposals with regard to consultation and co-operation between public authorities and employers' and workers' organisations at the industrial and national levels, which is the fifth item on the agenda of the session, and

Having determined that these proposals shall take the form of a Recommendation.

adopts this twentieth day of June of the year one thousand nine hundred and sixty and the following Recommendation, which may be cited as the Consultation (Industrial and National Levels) Recommendation, 1960:

1. (1) Measures appropriate to national conditions should be taken to promote effective consultation and co-operation at the industrial and national levels between public authorities and employers' and workers' organisations, as well as between these organisations, for the purposes indicated in Paragraphs 4 and 5 below, and on such other matters of mutual concern as the parties may determine.

(2) Such measures should be applied without discrimination of any kind against these organisations or amongst them on grounds such as the race, sex, religion, political opinion or national extraction of their members.

2. Such consultation and co-operation should not derogate from freedom of association or from the rights of employers' and workers' organisations, including their right of collective bargaining.

3. In accordance with national custom or practice, such consultation and co-operation should be provided for or facilitated:

(a) by voluntary action on the part of the employers' and workers' organisations, or

(b) by promotional action on the part of the public authorities, or

(c) by laws or regulations, or

(d) by a combination of any of these methods.

4. Such consultation and co-operation should have the general objective of promoting mutual understanding and good relations between public authorities and employers' and workers' organisations, as well as between these organisations, with a view to developing the economy as a whole or individual branches thereof, improving conditions of work and raising standards of living.

5. Such consultation and co-operation should aim, in particular:

(a) at joint consideration by employers' and workers' organisations of matters of mutual concern with a view to arriving, to the fullest possible extent, at agreed solutions; and

(b) at ensuring that the competent public authorities seek the views, advice and assistance of employers' and workers' organisations in an appropriate manner, in respect of such matters as:
   (i) the preparation and implementation of laws and regulations affecting their interests;
   (ii) the establishment and functioning of national bodies, such as those responsible for organisation of employment, vocational training and retraining, labour protection, industrial health and safety, productivity, social security and welfare; and
   (iii) the elaboration and implementation of plans of economic and social development.

## 2. Convention No. 144
### Tripartite Consultation (International Labour Standards), 1976

The General Conference of the International Labour Organisation,

Having been convened at Geneva by the Governing Body of the International Labour Office, and having met in its Sixty-first Session on 2 June 1976, and

Recalling the terms of existing international labour Conventions and Recommendations—in particular the Freedom of Association and Protection of the Right to Organise Convention, 1948, the Right to Organise and Collective Bargaining Convention, 1949, and the Consultation (Industrial and National Levels) Recommendation, 1960—which affirm the right of employers and workers to establish free and independent organisations and call for measures to promote effective consultation at the national level between public authorities and employers' and workers' organisations, as well as the provisions of numerous international labour Conventions and Recommendations which provide for the consultation of employers' and workers' organisations on measures to give effect thereto, and

Having considered the fourth item on the agenda of the session which is entitled "Establishment of tripartite machinery to promote the implementation of international labour standards", and having decided upon the adoption of certain proposals concerning tripartite consultations to promote the implementation of international labour standards, and

Having determined that these proposals shall take the form of an international Convention,

adopts this twenty-first day of June of the year one thousand nine hundred and seventy-six the following Convention, which may be cited as the Tripartite Consultation (International Labour Standards) Convention, 1976:

### Article 1

In this Convention the term "representative organisations" means the most representative organisations of employers and workers enjoying the right of freedom of association.

## Article 2

1. Each Member of the International Labour Organisation which ratifies this Convention undertakes to operate procedures which ensure effective consultations, with respect to the matters concerning the activities of the International Labour Organisation set out in Article 5, paragraph 1, below, between representatives of the government, of employers and of workers.

2. The nature and form of the procedures provided for in paragraph 1 of this Article shall be determined in each country in accordance with national practice, after consultation with the representative organisations, where such organisations exist and such procedures have not yet been established.

## Article 3

1. The representatives of employers and workers for the purposes of the procedures provided for in this Convention shall be freely chosen by their representative organisations, where such organisations exist.

2. Employers and workers shall be represented on an equal footing on any bodies through which consultations are undertaken.

## Article 4

1. The competent authority shall assume responsibility for the administrative support of the procedures provided for in this Convention.

2. Appropriate arrangements shall be made between the competent authority and the representative organisations, where such organisations exist, for the financing of any necessary training of participants in these procedures.

## Article 5

1. The purpose of the procedures provided for in this Convention shall be consultations on—

(a) government replies to questionnaires concerning items on the agenda of the International Labour Conference and government comments on proposed texts to be discussed by the Conference;

(b) the proposals to be made to the competent authority or authorities in connection with the submission of Conventions and Recommendations pursuant to article 19 of the Constitution of the International Labour Organisation;

(c) the re-examination at appropriate intervals of unratified Conventions and of Recommendations to which effect has not yet been given, to consider what measures might be taken to promote their implementation and ratification as appropriate;

(d) questions arising out of reports to be made to the International Labour Office under article 22 of the Constitution of the International Labour Organisation;

(e) proposals for the denunciation of ratified Conventions.

2. In order to ensure adequate consideration of the matters referred to in paragraph 1 of this Article, consultations shall be undertaken at appropriate intervals fixed by agreement, but at least once a year.

*Article 6*

When this is considered appropriate after consultation with the representative organisations, where such organisations exist, the competent authority shall issue an annual report on the working of the procedures provided for in this Convention.

## 3. Recommendation No. 152
## Tripartite Consultation (Activities of the International Labour Organisation), 1976

The General Conference of the International Labour Organisation,

Having been convened at Geneva by the Governing Body of the International Labour Office, and having met in its Sixty-first Session on 2 June 1976, and

Recalling the terms of existing international labour Conventions and Recommendations—in particular the Freedom of Association and Protection of the Right to Organise Convention, 1948, the Right to Organise and Collective Bargaining Convention 1949, and the Consultation (Industrial and National Levels) Recommendation, 1960—which affirm the right of employers and workers to establish free and independent organisations and call for measures to promote effective consultation at the national level between public authorities and employers' and workers' organisations, as well as the provisions of numerous international labour Conventions and Recommendations which provide for the consultation of employers' and workers' organisations on measures to give effect thereto, and

Having considered the fourth item on the agenda of the session which is entitled "Establishment of tripartite machinery to promote the implementation of international labour standards", and having decided upon the adoption of certain proposals concerning tripartite consultations to promote the implementation of international labour standards and national action relating to the activities of the International Labour Organisation, and

Having determined that these proposals shall take the form of a Recommendation,

adopts this twenty-first day of June of the year one thousand nine hundred and seventy-six the following Recommendation, which may be cited as the Tripartite Consultation (Activities of the International Labour Organisation) Recommendation, 1976:

1. In this Recommendation the term "representative organisations" means the most representative organisations of employers and workers enjoying the right of freedom of association.

2. (1) Each Member of the International Labour Organisation should operate procedures which ensure effective consultations with respect to matters concerning the activities of the International Labour Organisation, in accordance with Paragraphs 5 to 7 of this Recommendation, between representatives of the government, of employers and of workers.

(2) The nature and form of the procedures provided for in subparagraph (1) of this Paragraph should be determined in each country in accordance with national practice, after consultation with the representative organisations where such procedures have not yet been established.

(3) For instance, consultations may be undertaken—

*(a)* through a committee specifically constituted for questions concerning the activities of the International Labour Organisation;

*(b)* through a body with general competence in the economic, social or labour field;

*(c)* through a number of bodies with special responsibility for particular subject areas; or

*(d)* through written communications, where those involved in the consultative procedures are agreed that such communications are appropriate and sufficient.

3. (1) The representatives of employers and workers for the purposes of the procedures provided for in this Recommendation should be freely chosen by their representative organisations.

(2) Employers and workers should be represented on an equal footing on any bodies through which consultations are undertaken.

(3) Measures should be taken, in co-operation with the employers' and workers' organisations concerned, to make available appropriate training to enable participants in the procedures to perform their functions effectively.

4. The competent authority should assume responsibility for the administrative support and financing of the procedures provided for in this Recommendation, including the financing of training programmes where necessary.

5. The purpose of the procedures provided for in this Recommendation should be consultations—

*(a)* on government replies to questionnaires concerning items on the agenda of the International Labour Conference and government comments on proposed texts to be discussed by the Conference;

*(b)* on the proposals to be made to the competent authority or authorities in connection with the submission of Conventions and Recommendations pursuant to article 19 of the Constitution of the International Labour Organisation;

*(c)* subject to national practice, on the preparation and implementation of legislative or other measures to give effect to international labour Conventions and Recommendations, in particular to ratified Conventions (including measures for the implementation of provisions concerning the consultation or collaboration of employers' and workers' representatives);

*(d)* on the re-examination at appropriate intervals of unratified Conventions and of Recommendations to which effect has not yet been given, to consider what measures might be taken to promote their implementation and ratification as appropriate;

*(e)* on questions arising out of reports to be made to the International Labour Office under articles 19 and 22 of the Constitution of the International Labour Organisation;

*(f)* on proposals for the denunciation of ratified Conventions.

6. The competent authority, after consultation with the representative organisations, should determine the extent to which these procedures should be used for the purpose of consultations on other matters of mutual concern, such as—

*(a)* the preparation, implementation and evaluation of technical co-operation activities in which the International Labour Organisation participates;

*(b)* the action to be taken in respect of resolutions and other conclusions adopted by the International Labour Conference, regional conferences, industrial committees and other meetings convened by the International Labour Organisation;

*(c)* the promotion of a better knowledge of the activities of the International Labour Organisation as an element for use in economic and social policies and programmes.

7. In order to ensure adequate consideration of the matters referred to in the preceding Paragraphs, consultations should be undertaken at appropriate intervals fixed by agreement, but at least once a year.

8. Measures appropriate to national conditions and practice should be taken to ensure co-ordination between the procedures provided for in this Recommendation and the activities of national bodies dealing with analogous questions.

9. When this is considered appropriate after consultation with the representative organisations, the competent authority should issue an annual report on the working of the procedures provided for in this Recommendation.

## Employment security

### 1. Convention No. 158
### Termination of Employment, 1982

The General Conference of the International Labour Organisation,

Having been convened at Geneva by the Governing Body of the International Labour Office, and having met in its Sixty-eighth Session on 2 June 1982, and

Noting the existing international standards contained in the Termination of Employment Recommendation, 1963, and

Noting that since the adoption of the Termination of Employment Recommendation, 1963, significant developments have occurred in the law and practice of many member States on the questions covered by that Recommendation, and

Considering that these developments have made it appropriate to adopt new international standards on the subject, particularly having regard to the serious problems in this field resulting from the economic difficulties and technological changes experienced in recent years in many countries,

Having decided upon the adoption of certain proposals with regard to termination of employment at the initiative of the employer, which is the fifth item on the agenda of the session, and

Having determined that these proposals shall take the form of an international Convention;

adopts this twenty-second day of June of the year one thousand nine hundred and eighty-two the following Convention, which may be cited as the Termination of Employment Convention, 1982:

### Part I. Methods of implementation, scope and definitions

#### Article 1

The provisions of this Convention shall, in so far as they are not otherwise made effective by means of collective agreements, arbitration awards or court decisions or in such other manner as may be consistent with national practice, be given effect by laws or regulations.

#### Article 2

1. This Convention applies to all branches of economic activity and to all employed persons.

2. A Member may exclude the following categories of employed persons from all or some of the provisions of this Convention:

(a) workers engaged under a contract of employment for a specified period of time or a specified task;
(b) workers serving a period of probation or a qualifying period of employment, determined in advance and of reasonable duration;
(c) workers engaged on a casual basis for a short period.

3. Adequate safeguards shall be provided against recourse to contracts of employment for a specified period of time the aim of which is to avoid the protection resulting from this Convention.

4. In so far as necessary, measures may be taken by the competent authority or through the appropriate machinery in a country, after consultation with the organisations of employers and workers concerned, where such exist, to exclude from the application of this Convention or certain provisions thereof categories of employed persons whose terms and conditions of employment are governed by special arrangements which as a whole provide protection that is at least equivalent to the protection afforded under the Convention.

5. In so far as necessary, measures may be taken by the competent authority or through the appropriate machinery in a country, after consultation with the organisations of employers and workers concerned, where such exist, to exclude from the application of this Convention or certain provisions thereof other limited categories of employed persons in respect of which special problems of a substantial nature arise in the light of the particular conditions of employment of the workers concerned or the size or nature of the undertaking that employs them.

6. Each Member which ratifies this Convention shall list in the first report on the application of the Convention submitted under article 22 of the Constitution of the International Labour Organisation any categories which may have been excluded in pursuance of Paragraphs 4 and 5 of this Article, giving the reasons for such exclusion, and shall state in subsequent reports the position of its law and practice regarding the categories excluded, and the extent to which effect has been given or is proposed to be given to the Convention in respect of such categories.

### Article 3

For the purpose of this Convention the terms "termination" and "termination of employment" mean termination of employment at the initiative of the employer.

## Part II. Standards of general application

### Division A. Justification for termination

### Article 4

The employment of a worker shall not be terminated unless there is a valid reason for such termination connected with the capacity or conduct of the worker or based on the operational requirements of the undertaking, establishment or service.

### Article 5

The following, inter alia, shall not constitute valid reasons for termination:
(a) union membership or participation in union activities outside working hours or, with the consent of the employer, within working hours;

*(b)* seeking office as, or acting or having acted in the capacity of, a workers' representative;
*(c)* the filing of a complaint or the participation in proceedings against an employer involving alleged violation of laws or regulations or recourse to competent administrative authorities;
*(d)* race, colour, sex, marital status, family responsibilities, pregnancy, religion, political opinion, national extraction or social origin;
*(e)* absence from work during maternity leave.

## Article 6

1. Temporary absence from work because of illness or injury shall not constitute a valid reason for termination.

2. The definition of what constitutes temporary absence from work, the extent to which medical certification shall be required and possible limitations to the application of paragraph 1 of this Article shall be determined in accordance with the methods of implementation referred to in Article 1 of this Convention.

### Division B. Procedure prior to or at the time of termination

## Article 7

The employment of a worker shall not be terminated for reasons related to the worker's conduct or performance before he is provided an opportunity to defend himself against the allegations made, unless the employer cannot reasonably be expected to provide this opportunity.

### Division C. Procedure of appeal against termination

## Article 8

1. A worker who considers that his employment has been unjustifiably terminated shall be entitled to appeal against that termination to an impartial body, such as a court, labour tribunal, arbitration committee or arbitrator.

2. Where termination has been authorised by a competent authority the application of paragraph 1 of this Article may be varied according to national law and practice.

3. A worker may be deemed to have waived his right to appeal against the termination of his employment if he has not exercised that right within a reasonable period of time after termination.

## Article 9

1. The bodies referred to in Article 8 of this Convention shall be empowered to examine the reasons given for the termination and the other circumstances relating to the case and to render a decision on whether the termination was justified.

2. In order for the worker not to have to bear alone the burden of proving that the termination was not justified, the methods of implementation referred to in Article 1 of this Convention shall provide for one or the other or both of the following possibilities:

(a) the burden of proving the existence of a valid reason for the termination as defined in Article 4 of this Convention shall rest on the employer;

(b) the bodies referred to in Article 8 of this Convention shall be empowered to reach a conclusion on the reason for the termination having regard to the evidence provided by the parties and according to procedures provided for by national law and practice.

3. In cases of termination stated to be for reasons based on the operational requirements of the undertaking, establishment or service, the bodies referred to in Article 8 of this Convention shall be empowered to determine whether the termination was indeed for these reasons, but the extent to which they shall also be empowered to decide whether these reasons are sufficient to justify that termination shall be determined by the methods of implementation referred to in Article 1 of this Convention.

## Article 10

If the bodies referred to in Article 8 of this Convention find that termination is unjustified and if they are not empowered or do not find it practicable, in accordance with national law and practice, to declare the termination invalid and/or order or propose reinstatement of the worker, they shall be empowered to order payment of adequate compensation or such other relief as may be deemed appropriate.

### Division D. Period of notice

## Article 11

A worker whose employment is to be terminated shall be entitled to a reasonable period of notice or compensation in lieu thereof, unless he is guilty of serious misconduct, that is, misconduct of such a nature that it would be unreasonable to require the employer to continue his employment during the notice period.

### Division E. Severance allowance and other income protection

## Article 12

1. A worker whose employment has been terminated shall be entitled, in accordance with national law and practice, to—

(a) a severance allowance or other separation benefits, the amount of which shall be based inter alia on length of service and the level of wages, and paid directly by the employer or by a fund constituted by employers' contributions; or *(b)* benefits from unemployment insurance or assistance or other forms of social security, such as old-age or invalidity benefits, under the normal conditions to which such benefits are subject; or

*(c)* a combination of such allowance and benefits.

2. A worker who does not fulfil the qualifying conditions for unemployment insurance or assistance under a scheme of general scope need not be paid any allowance or benefit referred to in paragraph 1, subparagraph *(a)*, of this Article solely because he is not receiving an unemployment benefit under paragraph 1, subparagraph *(b)*.

3. Provision may be made by the methods of implementation referred to in Article 1 of this Convention for loss of entitlement to the allowance or benefits referred to in paragraph 1, subparagraph *(a)*, of this Article in the event of termination for serious misconduct.

## Part III. Supplementary provisions concerning terminations of employment for economic, technological, structural or similar reasons

### Division A. Consultation of workers' representatives

### Article 13

1. When the employer contemplates terminations for reasons of an economic, technological, structural or similar nature, the employer shall:

*(a)* provide the workers' representatives concerned in good time with relevant information including the reasons for the terminations contemplated, the number and categories of workers likely to be affected and the period over which the terminations are intended to be carried out;

*(b)* give, in accordance with national law and practice, the workers' representatives concerned, as early as possible, an opportunity for consultation on measures to be taken to avert or to minimise the terminations and measures to mitigate the adverse effects of any terminations on the workers concerned such as finding alternative employment.

2. The applicability of paragraph 1 of this Article may be limited by the methods of implementation referred to in Article 1 of this Convention to cases in which the number of workers whose termination of employment is contemplated is at least a specified number or percentage of the workforce.

3. For the purposes of this Article the term "the workers' representatives concerned" means the workers' representatives recognised as such by national law or practice, in conformity with the Workers' Representatives Convention, 1971.

### Division B. Notification to the competent authority

### Article 14

1. When the employer contemplates terminations for reasons of an economic, technological, structural or similar nature, he shall notify, in accordance with

national law and practice, the competent authority thereof as early as possible, giving relevant information, including a written statement of the reasons for the terminations, the number and categories of workers likely to be affected and the period over which the terminations are intended to be carried out.

2. National laws or regulations may limit the applicability of paragraph 1 of this Article to cases in which the number of workers whose termination of employment is contemplated is at least a specified number or percentage of the workforce.

3. The employer shall notify the competent authority of the terminations referred to in paragraph 1 of this Article a minimum period of time before carrying out the terminations, such period to be specified by national laws or regulations.

## 2. Recommendation No. 166
## Termination of Employment, 1982

The General Conference of the International Labour Organisation,

Having been convened at Geneva by the Governing Body of the International Labour Office, and having met in its Sixty-eighth Session on 2 June 1982, and

Having decided upon the adoption of certain proposals with regard to termination of employment at the initiative of the employer, which is the fifth item on the agenda of the session, and

Having determined that these proposals shall take the form of a Recommendation supplementing the Termination of Employment Convention, 1982;

adopts this twenty-second day of June of the year one thousand nine hundred and eighty-two the following Recommendation, which may be cited as the Termination of Employment Recommendation, 1982:

### I. Methods of implementation, scope and definitions

1. The provisions of this Recommendation may be applied by national laws or regulations, collective agreements, works rules, arbitration awards or court decisions on in such other manner consistent with national practice as may be appropriate under national conditions.

2. (1) This Recommendation applies to all branches of economic activity and to all employed persons.

(2) A Member may exclude the following categories of employed persons from all or some of the provisions of this Recommendation:

(a) workers engaged under a contract of employment for a specified period of time or a specified task;

(b) workers serving a period of probation or a qualifying period of employment, determined in advance and of reasonable duration;

(c) workers engaged on a casual basis for a short period.

(3) In so far as necessary, measures may be taken by the competent authority or through the appropriate machinery in a country, after consultation with the organisations of employers and workers concerned, where such exist, to exclude from the application of this Recommendation or certain provisions thereof categories of

employed persons whose terms and conditions of employment are governed by special arrangements, which as a whole provide protection that is at least equivalent to the protection afforded under the Recommendation.

(4) In so far as necessary, measures may be taken by the competent authority or through the appropriate machinery in a country, after consultation with the organisations of employers and workers concerned, where such exist, to exclude from the application of this Recommendation or certain provisions thereof other limited categories of employed persons in respect of which special problems of a substantial nature arise in the light of the particular conditions of employment of the workers concerned or the size or nature of the undertaking that employs them.

3. (1) Adequate safeguards should be provided against recourse to contracts of employment for a specified period of time the aim of which is to avoid the protection resulting from the Termination of Employment Convention, 1982, and this Recommendation.

(2) To this end, for example, provision may be made for one or more of the following:
*(a)* limiting recourse to contracts for a specified period of time to cases in which, owing either to the nature of the work to be effected or to the circumstances under which it is to be effected or to the interests of the worker, the employment relationship cannot be of indeterminate duration;
*(b)* deeming contracts for a specified period of time, other than in the cases referred to in clause *(a)* of this subparagraph, to be contracts of employment of indeterminate duration;
*(c)* deeming contracts for a specified period of time, when renewed on one or more occasions, other than in the cases mentioned in clause *(a)* of this subparagraph, to be contracts of employment of indeterminate duration.

4. For the purpose of this Recommendation the terms "termination" and "termination of employment" mean termination of employment at the initiative of the employer.

## II. Standards of general application

### Justification for termination

5. In addition to the grounds referred to in Article 5 of the Termination of Employment Convention, 1982, the following should not constitute valid reasons for termination:
*(a)* age, subject to national law and practice regarding retirement;
*(b)* absence from work due to compulsory military service or other civic obligations, in accordance with national law and practice.

6. (1) Temporary absence from work because of illness or injury should not constitute a valid reason for termination.

(2) The definition of what constitutes temporary absence from work, the extent to which medical certification should be required and possible limitations to the application of subparagraph (1) of this Paragraph should be determined in

accordance with the methods of implementation referred to in Paragraph 1 of this Recommendation.

*Procedure prior to or at the time of termination*

7. The employment of a worker should not be terminated for misconduct of a kind that under national law or practice would justify termination only if repeated on one or more occasions, unless the employer has given the worker appropriate written warning.

8. The employment of a worker should not be terminated for unsatisfactory performance, unless the employer has given the worker appropriate instructions and written warning and the worker continues to perform his duties unsatisfactorily after a reasonable period of time for improvement has elapsed.

9. A worker should be entitled to be assisted by another person when defending himself, in accordance with Article 7 of the Termination of Employment Convention, 1982, against allegations regarding his conduct or performance liable to result in the termination of his employment; this right may be specified by the methods of implementation referred to in Paragraph 1 of this Recommendation.

10. The employer should be deemed to have waived his right to terminate the employment of a worker for misconduct if he has failed to do so within a reasonable period of time after he has knowledge of the misconduct.

11. The employer may consult workers' representatives before a final decision is taken on individual cases of termination of employment.

12. The employer should notify a worker in writing of a decision to terminate his employment.

13. (1) A worker who has been notified of termination of employment or whose employment has been terminated should be entitled to receive, on request, a written statement from his employer of the reason or reasons for the termination.

(2) Subparagraph (1) of this Paragraph need not be applied in the case of collective termination for the reasons referred to in Articles 13 and 14 of the Termination of Employment Convention, 1982, if the procedure provided for therein is followed.

*Procedure of appeal against termination*

14. Provision may be made for recourse to a procedure of conciliation before or during appeal proceedings against termination of employment.

15. Efforts should be made by public authorities, workers' representatives and organisations of workers to ensure that workers are fully informed of the possibilities of appeal at their disposal.

*Time off from work during the period of notice*

16. During the period of notice referred to in Article 11 of the Termination of Employment Convention, 1982, the worker should, for the purpose of seeking other employment, be entitled to a reasonable amount of time off without loss of pay, taken at times that are convenient to both parties.

### Certificate of employment

17. A worker whose employment has been terminated should be entitled to receive, on request, a certificate from the employer specifying only the dates of his engagement and termination of his employment and the type or types of work on which he was employed; nevertheless, and at the request of the worker, an evaluation of his conduct and performance may be given in this certificate or in a separate certificate.

### Severance allowance and other income protection

18. (1) A worker whose employment has been terminated should be entitled, in accordance with national law and practice, to—
*(a)* a severance allowance or other separation benefits, the amount of which should be based, inter alia, on length of service and the level of wages, and paid directly by the employer or by a fund constituted by employers' contributions; or
*(b)* benefits from unemployment insurance or assistance or other forms of social security, such as old-age or invalidity benefits, under the normal conditions to which such benefits are subject; or
*(c)* a combination of such allowance and benefits.

(2) A worker who does not fulfil the qualifying conditions for unemployment insurance or assistance under a scheme of general scope need not be paid any allowance or benefit referred to in subparagraph (1) *(a)* of this Paragraph solely because he is not receiving an unemployment benefit under subparagraph (1) *(b)*.

(3) Provision may be made by the methods of implementation referred to in Paragraph 1 of this Recommendation for loss of entitlement to the allowance or benefits referred to in subparagraph (1) *(a)* of this Paragraph in the event of termination for serious misconduct.

## III. Supplementary provisions concerning terminations of employment for economic, technological, structural or similar reasons

19. (1) All parties concerned should seek to avert or minimise as far as possible termination of employment for reasons of an economic, technological, structural or similar nature, without prejudice to the efficient operation of the undertaking, establishment or service, and to mitigate the adverse effects of any termination of employment for these reasons on the worker or workers concerned.

(2) Where appropriate, the competent authority should assist the parties in seeking solutions to the problems raised by the terminations contemplated.

### Consultations on major changes in the undertaking

20. (1) When the employer contemplates the introduction of major changes in production, programme, organisation, structure or technology that are likely to entail terminations, the employer should consult the workers' representatives concerned as early as possible on, inter alia, the introduction of such changes, the effects they

are likely to have and the measures for averting or mitigating the adverse effects of such changes.

(2) To enable the workers' representatives concerned to participate effectively in the consultations referred to in subparagraph (1) of this Paragraph, the employer should supply them in good time with all relevant information on the major changes contemplated and the effects they are likely to have.

(3) For the purposes of this Paragraph the term "the workers' representatives concerned" means the workers' representatives recognised as such by national law or practice, in conformity with the Workers' Representatives Convention, 1971.

*Measures to avert or minimise termination*

21. The measures which should be considered with a view to averting or minimising terminations of employment for reasons of an economic, technological, structural or similar nature might include, inter alia, restriction of hiring, spreading the workforce reduction over a certain period of time to permit natural reduction of the workforce, internal transfers, training and retraining, voluntary early retirement with appropriate income protection, restriction of overtime and reduction of normal hours of work.

22. Where it is considered that a temporary reduction of normal hours of work would be likely to avert or minimise terminations of employment due to temporary economic difficulties, consideration should be given to partial compensation for loss of wages for the normal hours not worked, financed by methods appropriate under national law and practice.

*Criteria for selection for termination*

23. (1) The selection by the employer of workers whose employment is to be terminated for reasons of an economic, technological, structural or similar nature should be made according to criteria, established wherever possible in advance, which give due weight both to the interests of the undertaking, establishment or service and to the interests of the workers.

(2) These criteria, their order of priority and their relative weight, should be determined by the methods of implementation referred to in Paragraph 1 of this Recommendation.

*Priority of rehiring*

24. (1) Workers whose employment has been terminated for reasons of an economic, technological, structural or similar nature, should be given a certain priority of rehiring if the employer again hires workers with comparable qualifications, subject to their having, within a given period from the time of their leaving, expressed a desire to be rehired.

(2) Such priority of rehiring may be limited to a specified period of time.

(3) The criteria for the priority of rehiring, the question of retention of rights–particularly seniority rights–in the event of rehiring, as well as the terms

governing the wages of rehired workers, should be determined according to the methods of implementation referred to in Paragraph 1 of this Recommendation.

*Mitigating the effects of termination*

25. (1) In the event of termination of employment for reasons of an economic, technological, structural or similar nature, the placement of the workers affected in suitable alternative employment as soon as possible, with training or retraining where appropriate, should be promoted by measures suitable to national circumstances, to be taken by the competent authority, where possible with the collaboration of the employer and the workers' representatives concerned.

(2) Where possible, the employer should assist the workers affected in the search for suitable alternative employment, for example through direct contacts with other employers.

(3) In assisting the workers affected in obtaining suitable alternative employment or training or retraining, regard may be had to the Human Resources Development Convention and Recommendation, 1975.

26. (1) With a view to mitigating the adverse effects of termination of employment for reasons of an economic, technological, structural or similar nature, consideration should be given to providing income protection during any course of training or retraining and partial or total reimbursement of expenses connected with training or retraining and with finding and taking up employment which requires a change of residence.

(2) The competent authority should consider providing financial resources to support in full or in part the measures referred to in subparagraph (1) of this Paragraph, in accordance with national law and practice.

## IV. Effect on earlier Recommendation

27. This Recommendation and the Termination of Employment Convention, 1982, supersede the Termination of Employment Recommendation, 1963.

## Remuneration

### 1. Convention No. 26
### Minimum Wage-Fixing Machinery, 1928[1]

The General Conference of the International Labour Organisation,

Having been convened at Geneva by the Governing Body of the International Labour Office, and having met in its Eleventh Session on 30 May 1928, and

Having decided upon the adoption of certain proposals with regard to minimum wage-fixing machinery, which is the first item on the agenda of the Session, and

Having determined that these proposals should take the form of an international Convention,

adopts this sixteenth day of June of the year one thousand nine hundred and twenty-eight the following Convention, which may be cited as the Minimum Wage-Fixing Machinery Convention, 1928, for ratification by the Members of the International Labour Organisation in accordance with the provisions of the Constitution of the International Labour Organisation:

#### Article 1

1. Each member of the International Labour Organisation which ratifies this Convention undertakes to create or maintain machinery whereby minimum rates of wages can be fixed for workers employed in certain of the trades or parts of trades (and in particular in home working trades) in which no arrangements exist for the effective regulation of wages by collective agreement or otherwise and wages are exceptionally low.

2. For the purpose of this Convention, the term "trades" includes manufacture and commerce.

#### Article 2

Each Member which ratifies this Convention shall be free to decide, after consultation with the organisations, if any, of workers and employers in the trade or part of trade concerned, in which trades or parts of trades, and in particular in which home working trades or parts of such trades, the minimum wage-fixing machinery referred to in Article 1 shall be applied.

#### Article 3

1. Each Member which ratifies this Convention shall be free to decide the

---

[1] Date of coming into force: 14 June 1930.

nature and form of the minimum wage-fixing machinery, and the methods to be followed in its operation:

2. Provided that—

(1) before the machinery is applied in a trade or part of trade, representatives of the employers and workers concerned, including representatives of their respective organisations, if any, shall be consulted as well as any other persons, being specially qualified for the purpose by their trade of functions, whom the competent authority deems it expedient to consult;

(2) the employers and workers concerned shall be associated in the operation of the machinery, in such manner and to such extent, but in any case in equal numbers and on equal terms, as may be determined by national laws or regulations;

(3) minimum rates of wages which have been fixed shall be binding on the employers and workers concerned so as not to be subject to abatement by them by individual agreement, nor, except with general or particular authorisation of the competent authority, by collective agreement.

*Article 4*

1. Each Member which ratifies this Convention shall take the necessary measures, by way of a system of supervision and sanctions, to ensure that the employers and workers concerned are informed of the minimum rates of wages in force and that wages are not paid at less than these rates in cases where they are applicable.

2. A worker to whom the minimum rates are applicable and who has been paid wages at less than these rates shall be entitled to recover, by judicial or other legalised proceedings, the amount by which he has been underpaid, subject to such limitation of time as may be determined by national laws or regulations.

*Article 5*

Each Member which ratifies this Convention shall communicate annually to the International Labour Office a general statement giving a list of the trades or parts of trades in which the minimum wage-fixing machinery has been applied, indicating the methods as well as the results of the application of the machinery and, in summary form, the approximate number of workers covered, the minimum rates of wages fixed, and the more important of the other conditions, if any, established relevant to the minimum rates.

## 2. Recommendation No. 30
## Minimum Wage-Fixing Machinery, 1928

The General Conference of the International Labour Organisation,

Having been convened at Geneva by the Governing Body of the International Labour Office, and having met in its Eleventh Session on 30 May 1928, and

Having decided upon the adoption of certain proposals with regard to minimum wage-fixing machinery, which is the first item on the agenda of the Session, and

Having determined that these proposals should take the form of a Recommendation,

adopts this sixteenth day of June of the year one thousand nine hundred and twenty-eight the following Recommendation, which may be cited as the Minimum Wage-Fixing Machinery Recommendation, 1928, to be submitted to the Members of the International Labour Organisation for consideration with a view to effect being given to it by national legislation or otherwise, in accordance with the provisions of the Constitution of the International Labour Organisation:

## A

The General Conference of the International Labour Organisation,

Having adopted a Convention concerning the creation of minimum wage-fixing machinery, and

Desiring to supplement this Convention by putting on record for the guidance of the Members certain general principles which, as present practice and experience show, produce the most satisfactory results,

Recommends that each Member should take the following principles and rules into consideration:

## I

(1) In order to ensure that each Member ratifying the Convention is in possession of the information necessary for a decision upon the application of minimum wage-fixing machinery, the wages actually paid and the arrangements, if any, for the regulation of wages should be ascertained in respect of any trade or part of trade to which employers or workers therein request the application of the machinery and furnish information which shows prima facie that no arrangements exist for the effective regulation of wages and that wages are exceptionally low.

(2) Without prejudice to the discretion left to the Members by the Convention to decide in which trades or parts of trades in their respective countries it is expedient to apply minimum wage-fixing machinery, special regard might usefully be had to trades or parts of trades in which women are ordinarily employed.

## II

(1) The minimum wage-fixing machinery, whatever form it may take (for instance, trade boards for individual trades, general boards for groups of trades, compulsory arbitration tribunals), should operate by way of investigation into the relevant conditions in the trade or part of trade concerned, and consultation with the interests primarily and principally affected, that is to say, the employers and workers in the trade or part of trade, whose views on all matters relating to the fixing of the minimum rates of wages should in any case be solicited and be given full and equal consideration.

(2) *(a)* To secure greater authority for the rates that may be fixed, it should be the general policy that the employers and workers concerned, through representatives equal in number or having equal voting strength, should jointly take a direct part in

the deliberations and decisions of the wage-fixing body; in any case, where representation is accorded to one side, the other side should be represented on the same footing. The wage-fixing body should also include one or more independent persons whose votes can ensure effective decisions being reached in the event of the votes of the employers' and workers' representatives being equally divided. Such independent persons should, as far as possible, be selected in agreement with or after consultation with the employers' and workers' representatives on the wage-fixing body.

*(b)* In order to ensure that the employers' and workers' representatives shall be persons having the confidence of those whose interests they respectively represent, the employers and workers concerned should be given a voice as far as is practicable in the circumstances in the selection of their representatives, and if any organisations of the employers and workers exist these should in any case be invited to submit names of persons recommended by them for appointment on the wage-fixing body.

*(c)* The independent person or persons mentioned in Paragraph *(a)* should be selected from among men or women recognised as possessing the necessary qualifications for their duties and as being dissociated from any interest in the trade or part of trade concerned which might be calculated to put their impartiality in question.

*(d)* Wherever a considerable proportion of women are employed, provision should be made as far as possible for the inclusion of women among the workers' representatives and of one or more women among the independent persons mentioned in paragraph *(a)*.

## III

For the purpose of determining the minimum rates of wages to be fixed, the wage-fixing body should in any case take account of the necessity of enabling the workers concerned to maintain a suitable standard of living. For this purpose regard should primarily be had to the rates of wages being paid for similar work in trades where the workers are adequately organised and have concluded effective collective agreements, or, if no such standard of reference is available in the circumstances, to the general level of wages prevailing in the country or in the particular locality.

Provision should be made for the review of the minimum rates of wages fixed by the wage-fixing bodies when this is desired by the workers or employers who are members of such bodies.

## IV

For effectively protecting the wages of the workers concerned and safeguarding the employers affected against the possibility of unfair competition, the measures to be taken to ensure that wages are not paid at less than the minimum rates which have been fixed should include:
*(a)* arrangements for informing the employers and workers of the rates in force;
*(b)* official supervision of the rates actually being paid; and
*(c)* penalties for infringements of the rates in force and measures for preventing such infringements.

(1) In order that the workers, who are less likely than the employers to have their own means of acquainting themselves with the wage-fixing body's decisions,

may be kept informed of the minimum rates at which they are to be paid, employers might be required to display full statements of the rates in force in readily accessible positions on the premises where the workers are employed, or in the case of home workers on the premises where the work is given out or returned on completion or wages paid.

(2) A sufficient staff of inspectors should be employed, with powers analogous to those proposed for factory inspectors in the Recommendation concerning the general principles for the organisation of systems of inspection adopted by the General Conference in 1923, to make investigations among the employers and workers concerned with a view to ascertaining whether the minimum rates in force are in fact being paid and taking such steps as may be authorised to deal with infringements of the rates.

As a means of enabling the inspectors adequately to carry out these duties, employers might be required to keep complete and authentic records of the wages paid by them, or in the case of home workers to keep a list of the workers with their addresses and provide them with wage books or other similar record containing such particulars as are necessary to ascertain if the wages actually paid correspond to the rates in force.

(3) In cases where the workers are not in general in a position individually to enforce, by judicial or other legalised proceedings, their rights to recover wages due at the minimum rates in force, such other measures should be provided as may be considered effective for preventing infringements of the rates.

## B

The General Conference of the International Labour Organisation thinks it right to call the attention of governments to the principle affirmed by article 41 of the Constitution of the International Labour Organisation that men and women should receive equal remuneration for work of equal value.[1]

## 3. Convention No. 95
## Protection of Wages, 1949

The General Conference of the International Labour Organisation,

Having been convened at Geneva by the Governing Body of the International Labour Office, and having met in its Thirty-second Session on 8 June 1949, and

Having decided upon the adoption of certain proposals concerning the protection of wages, which is the seventh item on the agenda of the session, and

Having determined that these proposals shall take the form of an international Convention,

adopts this first day of July of the year one thousand nine hundred and forty-nine the following Convention, which may be cited as the Protection of Wages Convention, 1949:

---

[1] This paragraph refers to the Constitution of the International Labour Organisation prior to its amendment in 1946. In the Constitution as amended in 1946 a reference to equal remuneration appears in the Preamble.

## Article 1

In this Convention, the term "wages" means remuneration or earnings, however designated or calculated, capable of being expressed in terms of money and fixed by mutual agreement or by national laws or regulations, which are payable in virtue of a written or unwritten contract of employment by an employer to an employed person for work done or to be done or for services rendered or to be rendered.

## Article 2

1. This Convention applies to all persons to whom wages are paid or payable.

2. The competent authority may, after consultation with the organisations of employers and employed persons directly concerned, if such exist, exclude from the application of all or any of the provisions of the Convention categories of persons whose circumstances and conditions of employment are such that the application to them of all or any of the said provisions would be inappropriate and who are not employed in manual labour or are employed in domestic service or work similar thereto.

3. Each Member shall indicate in its first annual report upon the application of this Convention submitted under article 22 of the Constitution of the International Labour Organisation any categories of persons which it proposes to exclude from the application of all or any of the provisions of the Convention in accordance with the provisions of the preceding paragraph; no Member shall, after the date of its annual report, make exclusions except in respect of categories of persons so indicated.

4. Each Member having indicated in its first annual report categories of persons which it proposes to exclude from the application of all or any of the provisions of the Convention shall indicate in subsequent annual reports any categories of persons in respect of which it renounces the right to have recourse to the provisions of paragraph 2 of this Article and any progress which may have been made with a view to the application of the Convention to such categories of persons.

## Article 3

1. Wages payable in money shall be paid only in legal tender, and payment in the form of promissory notes, vouchers or coupons, or in any other form alleged to represent legal tender, shall be prohibited.

2. The competent authority may permit or prescribe the payment of wages by bank cheque or postal cheque or money order in cases in which payment in this manner is customary or is necessary because of special circumstances, or where a collective agreement or arbitration award so provides, or, where not so provided, with the consent of the worker concerned.

## Article 4

1. National laws or regulations, collective agreements or arbitration awards may authorise the partial payment of wages in the form of allowances in kind in

industries or occupations in which payment in the form of such allowances is customary or desirable because of the nature of the industry or occupation concerned; the payment of wages in the form of liquor of high alcoholic content or of noxious drugs shall not be permitted in any circumstances.

2. In cases in which partial payment of wages in the form of allowances in kind is authorised, appropriate measures shall be taken to ensure that—
*(a)* such allowances are appropriate for the personal use and benefit of the worker and his family; and
*(b)* the value attributed to such allowances is fair and reasonable.

### Article 5

Wages shall be paid directly to the worker concerned except as may be otherwise provided by national laws or regulations, collective agreement or arbitration award or where the worker concerned has agreed to the contrary.

### Article 6

Employers shall be prohibited from limiting in any manner the freedom of the worker to dispose of his wages.

### Article 7

1. Where works stores for the sale of commodities to the workers are established or services are operated in connection with an undertaking, the workers concerned shall be free from any coercion to make use of such stores or services.

2. Where access to other stores or services is not possible, the competent authority shall take appropriate measures with the object of ensuring that goods are sold and services provided at fair and reasonable prices, or that stores established and services operated by the employer are not operated for the purpose of securing a profit but for the benefit of the workers concerned.

### Article 8

1. Deductions from wages shall be permitted only under conditions and to the extent prescribed by national laws or regulations or fixed by collective agreement or arbitration award.

2. Workers shall be informed, in the manner deemed most appropriate by the competent authority, of the conditions under which and the extent to which such deductions may be made.

### Article 9

Any deduction from wages with a view to ensuring a direct or indirect payment for the purpose of obtaining or retaining employment, made by a worker to an employer or his representative or to any intermediary (such as a labour contractor or recruiter), shall be prohibited.

## Article 10

1. Wages may be attached or assigned only in a manner and within limits prescribed by national laws or regulations.

2. Wages shall be protected against attachment or assignment to the extent deemed necessary for the maintenance of the worker and his family.

## Article 11

1. In the event of the bankruptcy or judicial liquidation of an undertaking, the workers employed therein shall be treated as privileged creditors either as regards wages due to them for service rendered during such a period prior to the bankruptcy or judicial liquidation as may be prescribed by national laws or regulations, or as regards wages up to a prescribed amount as may be determined by national laws or regulations.

2. Wages constituting a privileged debt shall be paid in full before ordinary creditors may establish any claim to a share of the assets.

3. The relative priority of wages constituting a privileged debt and other privileged debts shall be determined by national laws or regulations.

## Article 12

1. Wages shall be paid regularly. Except where other appropriate arrangements exist which ensure the payment of wages at regular intervals, the intervals for the payment of wages shall be prescribed by national laws or regulations or fixed by collective agreement or arbitration award.

2. Upon the termination of a contract of employment, a final settlement of all wages due shall be effected in accordance with national laws or regulations, collective agreement or arbitration award or, in the absence of any applicable law, regulation, agreement or award, within a reasonable period of time having regard to the terms of the contract.

## Article 13

1. The payment of wages where made in cash shall be made on working days only and at or near the workplace, except as may be otherwise provided by national laws or regulations, collective agreement or arbitration award, or where other arrangements known to the workers concerned are considered more appropriate.

2. Payment of wages in taverns or other similar establishments and, where necessary to prevent abuse, in shops or stores for the retail sale of merchandise and in places of amusement shall be prohibited except in the case of persons employed therein.

## Article 14

Where necessary, effective measures shall be taken to ensure that workers are informed, in an appropriate and easily understandable manner—

(a) before they enter employment and when any changes take place, of the conditions in respect of wages under which they are employed; and
(b) at the time of each payment of wages, of the particulars of their wages for the pay period concerned, in so far as such particulars may be subject to change.

### Article 15

The laws or regulations giving effect to the provisions of this Convention shall—
(a) be made available for the information of persons concerned;
(b) define the persons responsible for compliance therewith;
(c) prescribe adequate penalties or other appropriate remedies for any violation thereof;
(d) provide for the maintenance, in all appropriate cases, of adequate records in an approved form and manner.

## 4. Recommendation No. 85
## Protection of Wages, 1949

The General Conference of the International Labour Organisation,

Having been convened at Geneva by the Governing Body of the International Labour Office, and having met in its Thirty-second Session on 8 June 1949, and

Having decided upon the adoption of certain proposals concerning the protection of wages, which is the seventh item on the agenda of the session, and

Having decided that these proposals shall take the form of a Recommendation supplementing the Protection of Wages Convention, 1949,

adopts this first day of July of the year one thousand nine hundred and forty-nine the following Recommendation, which may be cited as the Protection of Wages Recommendation, 1949:

The Conference recommends that each Member should apply the following provisions as rapidly as national conditions allow and report to the International Labour Office as requested by the Governing Body concerning the measures taken to give effect thereto.

### I. Deductions from wages

1. All necessary measures should be taken to limit deductions from wages to the extent deemed to be necessary to safeguard the maintenance of the worker and his family.

2. (1) Deductions from wages for the reimbursement of loss of or damage to the products, goods or installations of the employer should be authorised only when loss or damage has been caused for which the worker concerned can be clearly shown to be responsible.

(2) The amount of such deductions should be fair and should not exceed the actual amount of the loss or damage.

(3) Before a decision to make such a deduction is taken, the worker concerned should be given a reasonable opportunity to show cause why the deduction should not be made.

3. Appropriate measures should be taken to limit deductions from wages in respect of tools, materials or equipment supplied by the employer to cases in which such deductions—

(a) are a recognised custom of the trade or occupation concerned; or
(b) are provided for by collective agreement or arbitration award; or
(c) are otherwise authorised by a procedure recognised by national laws or regulations.

## II. Periodicity of wage payments

4. The maximum intervals for the payment of wages should ensure that wages are paid—

(a) not less often than twice a month at intervals not exceeding sixteen days in the case of workers whose wages are calculated by the hour, day or week; and
(b) not less often than once a month in the case of employed persons whose remuneration is fixed on a monthly or annual basis.

5. (1) In the case of workers whose wages are calculated on a piece-work or output basis, the maximum intervals for the payment of wages should, so far as possible, be so fixed as to ensure that wages are paid not less often than twice a month at intervals not exceeding sixteen days.

(2) In the case of workers employed to perform a task the completion of which requires more than a fortnight, and in respect of whom intervals for the payment of wages are not otherwise fixed by collective agreement or arbitration award, appropriate measures should be taken to ensure—

(a) that payments are made on account, not less often than twice a month at intervals not exceeding sixteen days, in proportion to the amount of work completed; and
(b) that final settlement is made within a fortnight of the completion of the task.

## III. Notification to workers of wage conditions

6. The details of the wages conditions which should be brought to the knowledge of the workers should include, wherever appropriate, particulars concerning—

(a) the rates of wages payable;
(b) the method of calculation;
(c) the periodicity of wage payments;
(d) the place of payment; and
(e) the conditions under which deductions may be made.

## IV. Wages statements and payroll records

7. In all appropriate cases, workers should be informed, with each payment of wages, of the following particulars relating to the pay period concerned, in so far as such particulars may be subject to change:

(a) the gross amount of wages earned;

(b) any deduction which may have been made, including the reasons therefore and the amount thereof; and

(c) the net amount of wages due.

8. Employers should be required in appropriate cases to maintain records showing, in respect of each worker employed, the particulars specified in the preceding Paragraph.

## V. Association of workers in the administration of works stores

9. Appropriate measures should be taken to encourage arrangements for the association of representatives of the workers concerned, and more particularly members of works welfare committees or similar bodies where such bodies exist, in the general administration of works stores or similar services established in connection with an undertaking for the sale of commodities or provision of services to the workers thereof.

## 5. Convention No. 99
## Minimum Wage Fixing Machinery (Agriculture), 1951 [1]

The General Conference of the International Labour Organisation,

Having been convened at Geneva by the Governing Body of the International Labour Office, and having met in its Thirty-fourth Session on 6 June 1951, and

Having decided upon the adoption of certain proposals with regard to minimum wage fixing machinery in agriculture, which is the eighth item on the agenda of the session, and

Having determined that these proposals shall take the form of an international Convention,

adopts this twenty-eighth day of June of the year one thousand nine hundred and fifty-one the following Convention, which may be cited as the Minimum Wage Fixing Machinery (Agriculture) Convention, 1951:

### Article 1

1. Each Member of the International Labour Organisation which ratifies this Convention undertakes to create or maintain adequate machinery whereby minimum rates of wages can be fixed for workers employed in agricultural undertakings and related occupations.

---

[1] Date of coming into force: 23 August 1953.

2. Each Member which ratifies this Convention shall be free to determine, after consultation with the most representative organisations of employers and workers concerned, where such exist, to which undertakings, occupations and categories of persons the minimum wage fixing machinery referred to in the preceding paragraph shall be applied.

3. The competent authority may exclude from the application of all or any of the provisions of this Convention categories of persons whose conditions of employment render such provisions inapplicable to them, such as members of the farmer's family employed by him.

## Article 2

1. National laws or regulations, collective agreements or arbitration awards may authorise the partial payment of minimum wages in the form of allowances in kind in cases in which payment in the form of such allowances is customary or desirable.

2. In cases in which partial payment of minimum wages in the form of allowances in kind is authorised, appropriate measures shall be taken to ensure that—
 (a) such allowances are appropriate for the personal use and benefit of the worker and his family; and
 (b) the value attributed to such allowances is fair and reasonable.

## Article 3

1. Each Member which ratifies this Convention shall be free to decide subject to the conditions stated in the following paragraphs, the nature and form of the minimum wage fixing machinery, and the methods to be followed in its operation.

2. Before a decision is taken there shall be full preliminary consultation with the most representative organisations of employers and workers concerned, where such exist, and with any other persons specially qualified by their trade or functions whom the competent authority deems it useful to consult.

3. The employers and workers concerned shall take part in the operation of the minimum wage fixing machinery, or be consulted or have the right to be heard, in such manner and to such extent as may be determined by national laws or regulations but in any case on a basis of complete equality.

4. Minimum rates of wages which have been fixed shall be binding on the employers and workers concerned so as not to be subject to abatement.

5. The competent authority may permit exceptions to the minimum wage rates in individual cases, where necessary, to prevent curtailment of the opportunities of employment of physically or mentally handicapped workers.

## Article 4

1. Each Member which ratifies this Convention shall take the necessary measures to ensure that the employers and workers concerned are informed of the minimum rates of wages in force and that wages are not paid at less than these rates in

STANDARDS AND GUIDING PRINCIPLES

cases where they are applicable; these measures shall include such provision for supervision, inspection, and sanctions as may be necessary and appropriate to the conditions prevailing in agriculture in the country concerned.

2. A worker to whom the minimum rates are applicable and who has been paid wages at less than these rates shall be entitled to recover, by judicial or other appropriate proceedings, the amount by which he has been underpaid, subject to such limitation of time as may be determined by national laws or regulations.

*Article 5*

Each Member which ratifies this Convention shall communicate annually to the International Labour Office a general statement indicating the methods and the results of the application of the machinery and, in summary form, the occupations and approximate numbers of workers covered, the minimum rates of wages fixed, and the more important of the other conditions, if any, established relevant to the minimum rates.

## 6. Recommendation No. 89
## Minimum Wage Fixing Machinery (Agriculture), 1951

The General Conference of the International Labour Organisation,

Having been convened at Geneva by the Governing Body of the International Labour Office, and having met in its Thirty-fourth Session on 6 June 1951, and

Having decided upon the adoption of certain proposals with regard to minimum wage fixing machinery in agriculture, which is the eighth item on the agenda of the session, and

Having decided that these proposals shall take the form of a Recommendation supplementing the Minimum Wage Fixing Machinery (Agriculture) Convention, 1951,

adopts this twenty-eighth day of June of the year one thousand nine hundred and fifty-one the following Recommendation, which may be cited as the Minimum Wage Fixing Machinery (Agriculture) Recommendation, 1951:

The Conference recommends that each Member should apply the following provisions as rapidly as national conditions allow and report to the International Labour Office as requested by the Governing Body concerning the measures taken to give effect thereto.

1. For the purpose of determining minimum rates of wages to be fixed it is desirable that the wage fixing body should in any case take account of the necessity of enabling the workers concerned to maintain a suitable standard of living.

2. Among the factors which should be taken into consideration in the fixing of minimum wage rates are the following: the cost of living, fair and reasonable value of services rendered, wages paid for similar or comparable work under collective bargaining agreements in agriculture, and the general level of wages for work of a

comparable skill in other industries in the area where the workers are sufficiently organised.

## II

3. Whatever form it may assume, the minimum wage fixing machinery in agriculture should operate by way of investigation into conditions in agriculture and related occupations, and consultation with the parties who are primarily and principally concerned, namely employers and workers, or their most representative organisations, where such exist. The opinion of both parties should be sought on all questions concerning minimum wage fixing and full and equal consideration given to their opinion.

4. To secure greater authority for the rates that may be fixed, in cases where the machinery adopted for fixing minimum wages makes it possible, the workers and employers concerned should be enabled to participate directly and on an equal footing in the operation of such machinery through their representatives who should be equal in number or in any case have an equal number of votes.

5. In order that the employers' and workers' representatives should enjoy the confidence of those whose interest they respectively represent, in the case referred to in Paragraph 4 above, the employers and workers concerned should have the right in so far as circumstances permit, to participate in the nomination of the representatives, and if any organisations of employers and workers exist, these should in any case be invited to submit names of persons recommended by them for appointment on the wage fixing body.

6. In the case where the machinery for minimum wage fixing provides for the participation of independent persons, whether for arbitration or otherwise, these should be chosen from among men or women who are recognised as possessing the necessary qualifications for their duties and who have no such interest in agriculture or in any branch thereof as would give rise to doubt as to their impartiality.

## III

7. Provision should be made for a procedure for revising minimum wage rates at appropriate intervals.

## IV

8. For effectively protecting the wages of the workers concerned, the measures to be taken to ensure that wages are not paid at less than the minimum rates which have been fixed should include—
 (a) arrangements for giving publicity to the minimum wage rates in force, and in particular for informing the employers and workers concerned of these rates in the manner most appropriate to national circumstances;
 (b) official supervision of the rates actually being paid; and
 (c) penalties for infringements of the rates in force and measures for preventing such infringements.

9. A sufficient number of qualified inspectors, with powers analogous to those provided for in the Labour Inspection Convention, 1947, should be employed; these inspectors should make investigations among the employers and workers concerned with a view to ascertaining whether the wages actually paid are in conformity with the minimum rates in force and, if need be, should take such steps as may be authorised in the case of infringement of the rate fixed.

10. In order to enable the inspectors to carry out their duties efficiently, employers should, where appropriate or necessary in the opinion of the competent authority, be required to keep complete and authentic records of the wages paid by them, and might also be required to issue the workers pay books or similar documents containing the information necessary for verifying whether the wages actually paid correspond to the rates in force.

11. In cases where the workers are not in general in a position individually to enforce, by judicial or appropriate proceedings, their rights to recover wages due at the minimum rates in force, such other measures should be provided as may be considered effective for this purpose.

## 7. Convention No. 100
### Equal Remuneration, 1951

The General Conference of the International Labour Organisation,

Having been convened at Geneva by the Governing Body of the International Labour Office, and having met in its Thirty-fourth Session on 6 June 1951, and

Having decided upon the adoption of certain proposals with regard to the principle of equal remuneration for men and women workers for work of equal value, which is the seventh item on the agenda of the session, and

Having determined that these proposals shall take the form of an international Convention,

adopts this twenty-ninth day of June of the year one thousand nine hundred and fifty-one the following Convention, which may be cited as the Equal Remuneration Convention, 1951:

### Article 1

For the purpose of this Convention—

(a) the term "remuneration" includes the ordinary, basic or minimum wage or salary and any additional emoluments whatsoever payable directly or indirectly, whether in cash or in kind, by the employer to the worker and arising out of the worker's employment;

(b) the term "equal remuneration for men and women workers for work of equal value" refers to rates of remuneration established without discrimination based on sex.

### Article 2

1. Each Member shall, by means appropriate to the methods in operation for determining rates of remuneration, promote and, in so far as is consistent with such

methods, ensure the application to all workers of the principle of equal remuneration for men and women workers for work of equal value.

2. This principle may be applied by means of—
*(a)* national laws or regulations;
*(b)* legally established or recognised machinery for wage determination;
*(c)* collective agreements between employers and workers; or
*(d)* a combination of these various means.

### Article 3

1. Where such action will assist in giving effect to the provisions of this Convention measures shall be taken to promote objective appraisal of jobs on the basis of the work to be performed.

2. The methods to be followed in this appraisal may be decided upon by the authorities responsible for the determination of rates of remuneration, or, where such rates are determined by collective agreements, by the parties thereto.

3. Differential rates between workers which correspond, without regard to sex, to differences, as determined by such objective appraisal, in the work to be performed shall not be considered as being contrary to the principle of equal remuneration for men and women workers for work of equal value.

### Article 4

Each Member shall co-operate as appropriate with the employers' and workers' organisations concerned for the purpose of giving effect to the provisions of this Convention.

## 8. Recommendation No. 90
## Equal Remuneration, 1951

The General Conference of the International Labour Organisation,

Having been convened at Geneva by the Governing Body of the International Labour Office, and having met in its Thirty-fourth Session on 6 June 1951, and

Having decided upon the adoption of certain proposals with regard to the principle of equal remuneration for men and women workers for work of equal value, which is the seventh item on the agenda of the session, and

Having determined that these proposals shall take the form of a Recommendation supplementing the Equal Remuneration Convention, 1951,

adopts this twenty-ninth day of June of the year one thousand nine hundred and fifty-one the following Recommendation, which may be cited as the Equal Remuneration Recommendation, 1951;

Whereas the Equal Remuneration Convention, 1951, lays down certain general principles concerning equal remuneration for men and women workers for work of equal value;

Whereas the Convention provides that the application of the principle of equal remuneration for men and women workers for work of equal value shall be promoted or ensured by means appropriate to the methods in operation for determining rates of remuneration in the countries concerned;

Whereas it is desirable to indicate certain procedures for the progressive application of the principles laid down in the Convention;

Whereas it is at the same time desirable that all Members should, in applying these principles, have regard to methods of application which have been found satisfactory in certain countries;

The Conference recommends that each Member should, subject to the provisions of Article 2 of the Convention, apply the following provisions and report to the International Labour Office as requested by the Governing Body concerning the measures taken to give effect thereto:

1. Appropriate action should be be taken, after consultation with the workers' organisations concerned or, where such organisations do not exist, with the workers concerned—

(a) to ensure the application of the principle of equal remuneration for men and women workers for work of equal value to all employees of central Government departments or agencies; and

(b) to encourage the application of the principle to employees of State, provincial or local Government departments or agencies, where these have jurisdiction over rates of remuneration.

2. Appropriate action should be taken, after consultation with the employers' and workers' organisations concerned, to ensure, as rapidly as practicable, the application of the principle of equal remuneration for men and women workers for work of equal value in all occupations, other than those mentioned in Paragraph 1, in which rates of remuneration are subject to statutory regulation or public control, particularly as regards—

(a) the establishment of minimum or other wage rates in industries and services where such rates are determined under public authority;

(b) industries and undertakings operated under public ownership or control; and

(c) where appropriate, work executed under the terms of public contracts.

3. (1) Where appropriate in the light of the methods in operation for the determination of rates of remuneration, provision should be made by legal enactment for the general application of the principle of equal remuneration for men and women workers for work of equal value.

(2) The competent public authority should take all necessary and appropriate measures to ensure that employers and workers are fully informed as to such legal requirements and, where appropriate, advised on their application.

4. When, after consultation with the organisations of workers and employers concerned, where such exist, it is not deemed feasible to implement immediately the principle of equal remuneration for men and women workers for work of equal value, in respect of employment covered by Paragraph 1, 2 or 3, appropriate provision should be made or caused to be made, as soon as possible, for its progressive application, by such measures as—

(a) decreasing the differentials between rates of remuneration for men and rates of remuneration for women for work of equal value;

*(b)* where a system of increments is in force, providing equal increments for men and women workers performing work of equal value.

5. Where appropriate for the purpose of facilitating the determination of rates or remuneration in accordance with the principle of equal remuneration for men and women workers for work of equal value, each Member should, in agreement with the employers' and workers' organisations concerned, establish or encourage the establishment of methods for objective appraisal of the work to be performed, whether by job analysis or by other procedures, with a view to providing a classification of jobs without regard to sex; such methods should be applied in accordance with the provisions of Article 2 of the Convention.

6. In order to facilitate the application of the principle of equal remuneration for men and women workers for work of equal value, appropriate action should be taken, where necessary to raise the productive efficiency of women workers by such measures as—

*(a)* ensuring that workers of both sexes have equal or equivalent facilities for vocational guidance or employment counselling, for vocational training and for placement;

*(b)* taking appropriate measures to encourage women to use facilities for vocational guidance or employment counselling, for vocational training and for placement;

*(c)* providing welfare and social services which meet the needs of women workers, particularly those with family responsibilities, and financing such services from general public funds or from social security or industrial welfare funds financed by payments made in respect of workers without regard to sex; and

*(d)* promoting equality of men and women workers as regards access to occupations and posts without prejudice to the provisions of international regulations and of national laws and regulations concerning the protection of the health and welfare of women.

7. Every effort should be made to promote public understanding of the grounds on which it is considered that the principle of equal remuneration for men and women workers for work of equal value should be implemented.

8. Such investigations as may be desirable to promote the application of the principle should be undertaken.

## 9. Convention No. 131
## Minimum Wage Fixing, 1970

The General Conference of the International Labour Organisation,

Having been convened at Geneva by the Governing Body of the International Labour Office, and having met in its Fifty-fourth Session on 3 June 1970, and

Noting the terms of the Minimum Wage-Fixing Machinery Convention, 1928 and the Equal Remuneration Convention, 1951, which have been widely ratified, as well as of the Minimum Wage Fixing Machinery (Agriculture) Convention, 1951, and

Considering that these Conventions have played a valuable part in protecting disadvantaged groups of wage earners, and

Considering that the time has come to adopt a further instrument complementing these Conventions and providing protection for wage earners against unduly low wages, which, while of general application, pays special regard to the needs of developing countries, and

Having decided upon the adoption of certain proposals with regard to minimum wage fixing machinery, and related problems, with special reference to developing countries, which is the fifth item on the agenda of the session, and

Having determined that these proposals shall take the form of an international Convention,

adopts this twenty-second day of June of the year one thousand nine hundred and seventy the following Convention, which may be cited as the Minimum Wage Fixing Convention, 1970:

## Article 1

1. Each Member of the International Labour Organisation which ratifies this Convention undertakes to establish a system of minimum wages which covers all groups of wage earners whose terms of employment are such that coverage would be appropriate.

2. The competent authority in each country shall, in agreement or after full consultation with the representative organisations of employers and workers concerned, where such exist, determine the groups of wage earners to be covered.

3. Each Member which ratifies this Convention shall list in the first report on the application of the Convention submitted under article 22 of the Constitution of the International Labour Organisation any groups of wage earners which may not have been covered in pursuance of this Article, giving the reasons for not covering them, and shall state in subsequent reports the position of its law and practice in respect of the groups not covered, and the extent to which effect has been given or is proposed to be given to the Convention in respect of such groups.

## Article 2

1. Minimum wages shall have the force of law and shall not be subject to abatement, and failure to apply them shall make the person or persons concerned liable to appropriate penal or other sanctions.

2. Subject to the provisions of paragraph 1 of this Article, the freedom of collective bargaining shall be fully respected.

## Article 3

The elements to be taken into consideration in determining the level of minimum wages shall, so far as possible and appropriate in relation to national practice and conditions, include—

(a) the needs of workers and their families, taking into account the general level of wages in the country, the cost of living, social security benefits, and the relative living standards of other social groups;

(b) economic factors, including the requirements of economic development, levels of productivity and the desirability of attaining and maintaining a high level of employment.

## Article 4

1. Each Member which ratifies this Convention shall create and/or maintain machinery adapted to national conditions and requirements whereby minimum wages for groups of wage earners covered in pursuance of Article 1 thereof can be fixed and adjusted from time to time.

2. Provision shall be made, in connection with the establishment, operation and modification of such machinery, for full consultation with representative organisations of employers and workers concerned or, where no such organisations exist, representatives of employers and workers concerned.

3. Wherever it is appropriate to the nature of the minimum wage fixing machinery, provision shall also be made for the direct participation in its operation of—

(a) representatives of organisations of employers and workers concerned or, where no such organisations exist, representatives of employers and workers concerned, on a basis of equality;

(b) persons having recognised competence for representing the general interests of the country and appointed after full consultation with representative organisations of employers and workers concerned, where such organisations exist and such consultation is in accordance with national law or practice.

## Article 5

Appropriate measures, such as adequate inspection reinforced by other necessary measures, shall be taken to ensure the effective application of all provisions relating to minimum wages.

## Article 6

This Convention shall not be regarded as revising any existing Convention.

## 10. Recommendation No. 135
## Minimum Wage Fixing, 1970

The General Conference of the International Labour Organisation,

Having been convened at Geneva by the Governing Body of the International Labour Office, and having met in its Fifty-fourth Session on 3 June 1970, and

Noting the Terms of the Minimum Wage Fixing Machinery Recommendation, 1928, the Minimum Wage Fixing Machinery (Agriculture) Recommendation, 1951, and the Equal Remuneration Recommendation, 1951, which contain valuable guidelines for minimum wage fixing bodies, and

Considering that experience in more recent years has emphasised the importance of certain additional considerations relating to minimum wage fixing, including that of adopting criteria which will make systems of minimum wages both an effective instrument of social protection and an element in the strategy of economic and social development, and

Considering that minimum wage fixing should in no way operate to the prejudice of the exercise and growth of free collective bargaining as a means of fixing wages higher than the minimum, and

Having decided upon the adoption of certain proposals with regard to minimum wage fixing machinery and related problems, with special reference to developing countries, which is the fifth item on the agenda of the session, and

Having determined that these proposals shall take the form of a Recommendation,

adopts this twenty-second day of June of the year one thousand nine hundred and seventy the following Recommendation, which may be cited as the Minimum Wage Fixing Recommendation, 1970:

## I. Purpose of minimum wage fixing

1. Minimum wage fixing should constitute one element in a policy designed to overcome poverty and to ensure the satisfaction of the needs of all workers and their families.

2. The fundamental purpose of minimum wage fixing should be to give wage earners necessary social protection as regards minimum permissible levels of wages.

## II. Criteria for determining the level of minimum wages

3. In determining the level of minimum wages, account should be taken of the following criteria, amongst others:
*(a)* the needs of workers and their families;
*(b)* the general level of wages in the country;
*(c)* the cost of living and changes therein;
*(d)* social security benefits;
*(e)* the relative living standards of other social groups;
*(f)* economic factors, including the requirements of economic development, levels of productivity and the desirability of attaining and maintaining a high level of employment.

## III. Coverage of the minimum wage fixing system

4. The number and groups of wage earners who are not covered in pursuance of Article 1 of the Minimum Wage Fixing Convention, 1970, should be kept to a minimum.

5. (1) The system of minimum wages may be applied to the wage earners covered in pursuance of Article 1 of the Convention either by fixing a single minimum wage of general application or by fixing a series of minimum wages applying to particular groups of workers.

(2) A system based on a single minimum wage—

(a) need not be incompatible with the fixing of different rates of minimum wages in different regions or zones with a view to allowing for differences in costs of living;

(b) should not impair the effects of decisions, past or future, fixing minimum wages higher than the general minimum for particular groups of workers.

## IV. Minimum wage fixing machinery

6. The minimum wage fixing machinery provided for in Article 4 of the Convention may take a variety of forms, such as the fixing of minimum wages by—

(a) statute;

(b) decisions of the competent authority, with or without formal provision for taking account of recommendations from other bodies;

(c) decisions of wages boards or councils;

(d) industrial or labour courts or tribunals; or

(e) giving the force of law to provisions of collective agreements.

7. The consultation provided for in paragraph 2 of Article 4 of the Convention should include, in particular, consultation in regard to the following matters:

(a) the selection and application of the criteria for determining the level of minimum wages;

(b) the rate or rates of minimum wages to be fixed;

(c) the adjustment from time to time of the rate or rates of minimum wages;

(d) problems encountered in the enforcement of minimum wage legislation;

(e) the collection of data and the carrying out of studies for the information of minimum wage fixing authorities.

8. In countries in which bodies have been set up which advise the competent authority on minimum wage questions, or to which the government has delegated responsibility for minimum wage decisions, the participation in the operation of minimum wage fixing machinery referred to in paragraph 3 of Article 4 of the Convention should include membership of such bodies.

9. The persons representing the general interests of the country whose participation in the operation of minimum wage fixing machinery is provided for in Article 4, paragraph 3, subparagraph (b) of the Convention should be suitably qualified independent persons who may, where appropriate, be public officials with responsibilities in the areas of industrial relations or economic and social planning or policy-making.

10. To the extent possible in national circumstances, sufficient resources should be devoted to the collection of statistics and other data needed for analytical studies of the relevant economic factors, particularly those mentioned in Paragraph 3 of this Recommendation, and their probable evolution.

## V. Adjustment of minimum wages

11. Minimum wage rates should be adjusted from time to time to take account of changes in the cost of living and other economic conditions.

12. To this end a review might be carried out of minimum wage rates in relation to the cost of living and other economic conditions either at regular intervals or whenever such a review is considered appropriate in the light of variations in a cost-of-living index.

13. (1) In order to assist in the application of Paragraph 11 of this Recommendation, periodical surveys of national economic conditions, including trends in income per head, in productivity and in employment, unemployment and underemployment, should be made to the extent that national resources permit.

(2) The frequency of such surveys should be determined in the light of national conditions.

## VI. Enforcement

14. Measures to ensure the effective application of all provisions relating to minimum wages, as provided for in Article 5 of the Convention, should include the following:

(a) arrangements for giving publicity to minimum wage provisions in languages or dialects understood by workers who need protection, adapted where necessary to the needs of illiterate persons;

(b) the employment of a sufficient number of adequately trained inspectors equipped with the powers and facilities necessary to carry out their duties;

(c) adequate penalties for infringement of the provisions relating to minimum wages;

(d) simplification of legal provisions and procedures, and other appropriate means of enabling workers effectively to exercise their rights under minimum wage provisions, including the right to recover amounts by which they may have been underpaid;

(e) the association of employers' and workers' organisations in efforts to protect workers against abuses;

(f) adequate protection of workers against victimisation.

Part II

*Other instruments*

# A. Resolutions adopted by the International Labour Conference

## 1. Trade union rights and their relation to civil liberties

The General Conference of the International Labour Organisation,

Considering that the Preamble of the Constitution of the International Labour Organisation proclaims recognition of the principle of freedom of association as one of the objectives of the Organisation,

Considering that the Declaration of Philadelphia, an integral part of the Constitution, proclaims that freedom of expression and of association are essential to sustained progress and refers to other fundamental human rights inherent in human dignity,

Considering that the International Labour Organisation has laid down basic standards of freedom of association for trade union purposes in the Freedom of Association and Protection of the Right to Organise Convention, 1948 (No. 87), and the Right to Organise and Collective Bargaining Convention, 1949 (No. 98),

Considering that without national independence and political liberty full and genuine trade union rights could not exist,

Considering that trade unions, provided they enjoy their full rights, are an essential factor for the attainment of the objective of economic, social and cultural progress stated in the Constitution of the ILO,

Considering that the rights of workers' and employers' organisations and of human beings in general flourish in a climate of social and economic progress,

Considering that the advancement of the rights of workers' and employers' organisations is linked both to national social and economic development and to national, regional and international legislation,

Considering that, according to Article 8 of the Freedom of Association and Protection of the Right to Organise Convention, 1948, workers, employers and their organisations should respect the law of the land in exercising the rights provided for in that Convention, but the law of the land should not be such as to impair, nor should it be so applied as to impair, the guarantees provided for in the Convention, and that this principle should also be respected when trade unions assume responsibility in the interests of the common welfare,

Recalling earlier calls by the Conference for reinforcing the action and machinery of the International Labour Organisation for the protection of trade union rights, more particularly the resolution concerning freedom of association, adopted on 9 July 1964, and the resolution concerning action by the International Labour Organisation in the field of human rights and in particular with respect to freedom of association, adopted on 24 June 1968,

Considering the evolution which has taken place in various fields and the fact that the present session of the Conference has dealt with the question of protection and facilities afforded to workers' representatives,

Regretting that forty-five Members of the International Labour Organisation have not yet ratified the Freedom of Association and Protection of the Right to Organise Convention, 1948, and that thirty-two Members have not yet ratified the Right to Organise and Collective Bargaining Convention, 1949, and deploring that some of these States violate and infringe the principles laid down in these instruments,

Deploring also that amongst the member States which have ratified these Conventions some do not yet apply them fully and others violate them,

Considering that the supervisory machinery of the ILO, and particularly the Governing Body Committee on Freedom of Association, on the basis of existing standards, has taken supplementary decisions concerning infringements of trade union rights which refer also to specific civil liberties,

Considering that the possibilities of protecting trade union rights would be strengthened if the ILO gave the widest publicity to these decisions,

Considering that the question of the protection of civil liberties as such comes within the purview of the United Nations on the basis of the Universal Declaration of Human Rights and the International Covenants on Civil and Political Rights and on Economic, Social and Cultural Rights, and that the speedy ratification and application of these Covenants is of the utmost importance as a means of reinforcing the protection of trade union rights,

Considering that there exist firmly established, universally recognised principles defining the basic guarantees of civil liberties which should constitute a common standard of achievement for all peoples and all nations, enunciated in particular in the Universal Declaration of Human Rights and the International Covenants on Human Rights, but that the observance of the standards embodied in the Covenants will become a binding obligation for States only when the Covenants are ratified and enter into force,

Considering that war, colonial or neo-colonial domination and racial discrimination are major obstacles to the welfare of workers and a flagrant impediment to the work of the International Labour Organisation,

Considering that international measures to provide more effective protection for specific civil liberties by the United Nations would reinforce the action of the International Labour Organisation for the protection of trade union rights;

1. Recognises that the rights conferred upon workers' and employers' organisations must be based on respect for those civil liberties which have been enunciated in particular in the Universal Declaration of Human Rights and in the International Covenants on Civil and Political Rights and that the absence of these civil liberties removes all meaning from the concept of trade union rights.

2. Places special emphasis on the following civil liberties, as defined in the Universal Declaration of Human Rights, which are essential for the normal exercise of trade union rights:

*(a)* the right to freedom and security of person and freedom from arbitrary arrest and detention;

*(b)* freedom of opinion and expression and in particular freedom to hold opinions without interference and to seek, receive and impart information and ideas through any media and regardless of frontiers;

*(c)* freedom of assembly;
*(d)* the right to a fair trial by an independent and impartial tribunal;
*(e)* the right to protection of the property of trade union organisations.

3. Reaffirms the ILO's specific competence–within the United Nations system–in the field of freedom of association and trade union rights (principles, standards, supervisory machinery) and of related civil liberties.

4. Emphasises the responsibility of the United Nations for protecting and promoting human rights in general, political freedoms and civil liberties throughout the world.

5. Expresses its deep concern about and condemns the repeated violations of trade union rights and other human rights.

6. Calls upon all member States which have not done so to ratify and apply the United Nations Covenants on Civil and Political Rights and on Economic, Social and Cultural Rights, and invites the United Nations also to seek this.

7. Invites the Governing Body to pursue energetically the efforts of the ILO with a view to total decolonisation along the lines of the Declaration adopted on this subject by the United Nations.

8. Invites the Governing Body to extend and expand its efforts to eliminate the discriminatory practices on the basis of race, colour, sex, religion, nationality, political and trade union opinion which still exist in several countries, including countries and territories under a colonial regime or foreign domination in any form.

9. Reaffirms its belief in the principles which inspired the Freedom of Association and Protection of the Right to Organise Convention, 1948 (No. 87), and the Right to Organise and Collective Bargaining Convention, 1949 (No. 98), and strongly urges that all member States which have not already done so to ratify these Conventions and, pending ratification, that they ensure that the principles embodied in these Conventions are observed and that they respect the principles enshrined in these Conventions in the enactment of their national legislation.

10. Invites the Governing Body of the ILO to take as soon as possible the necessary steps, pursuant to the resolution of 1964, with a view to including in the Constitution of the ILO the essential principles contained in these Conventions concerning trade union freedom.

11. Invites the Governing Body to instruct the Director-General to publish and distribute widely in a concise form the supplementary decisions taken by the Committee on Freedom of Association.

12. Invites the Governing Body to ensure wider knowledge of ILO principles and standards concerning trade union rights, using to this end, in particular, regional conferences, seminars, programmes for workers' and management education, etc.

13. Invites the Director-General of the ILO to express the support of the ILO for the action of the United Nations in the field of human rights and to draw the attention of the appropriate United Nations bodies to the relationship which exists between trade union rights and civil liberties.

14. Invites the Governing Body to undertake all efforts with a view to strengthening the ILO machinery for securing the observance by member States of ILO principles concerning freedom of association and trade union rights.

15. Invites the Governing Body to instruct the Director-General to undertake further comprehensive studies and to prepare reports on law and practice in matters concerning freedom of association and trade union rights and related civil liberties falling within the competence of the ILO, with a view to considering further action to ensure full and universal respect for trade union rights in their broadest sense;

For this purpose particular attention should be given to the following questions:

- right of trade unions to exercise their activities in the undertaking and other workplaces;
- right of trade unions to negotiate wages and all other conditions of work;
- right to participation of trade unions in undertakings and in the general economy;
- right to strike;
- right to participate fully in national and international trade union activities;
- right to inviolability of trade union premises as well as of correspondence and telephonic conversations;
- right to protection of trade union funds and assets against intervention by the public authorities;
- right of trade unions to have access to media of mass communication;
- right to protection against any discrimination in matters of affiliation and trade union activities;
- right of access to voluntary conciliation and arbitration procedures;
- right to workers' education and further training.

16. Invites the Governing Body, taking into account the studies and reports prepared by the ILO, to place on the agenda of a forthcoming session of the International Labour Conference one or more questions which could be the subject of new instruments with a view to enlarging trade union rights, taking into account those civil liberties which are a prerequisite for their exercise.

54th Session, 1970

## 2. Labour and Social Implications of Automation and Other Technological Developments

The General Conference of the International Labour Organisation,

Noting that automation and modern technology, and the resulting technological change, have often brought widespread social and economic gains to all strata of society in both developing and industrialised countries and offer the promise of providing ever greater benefits and opportunities,

Concerned that the advantages of new technology should not be overshadowed by harmful effects which would arise from ill-planned introduction and application,

Convinced that the benefits of advanced technology should be widely shared by all members of society rather than accrue only to the workers and employers directly involved, and that hardships resulting from technological change should not affect a few heavily but should be shared by the community as a whole,

Considering that the Declaration of Philadelphia states that the ILO should promote, among other objectives, the adoption of national programmes which will achieve: full employment and the improvement of living conditions; work opportunities offering workers assurance of being able to make full use of their skills and knowledge; the provision for workers of a fair share of the fruits of progress as regards income and wages, working hours and other conditions of employment; co-operation between employers and workers with a view to the steady growth of productivity and the planning and implementation of social and economic action; and the expansion of social security protection,

Observing that technological developments may in some cases result in negative economic, social and individual consequences which may jeopardise the attainment of the principles set forth in the Declaration of Philadelphia,

Recognising that in view of the wide-ranging social and economic effects of advanced technology, decisions concerning its introduction may, depending on the magnitude of the change and national custom and practice, require the participation of government agencies,

Recalling that at previous sessions the International Labour Conference has considered the problem, in particular at the 39th (1956) Session, when it adopted a resolution concerning future ILO action on automation questions and at the 40th (1957) Session, to which the Director-General submitted a report on automation and other technological developments,

Noting with satisfaction that since that time the ILO has undertaken numerous activities involving consideration of the social problems associated with technological development and programmes to reduce the hardships arising from such problems,

Recalling in particular the conclusions and recommendations adopted in 1967 by the meeting of experts on programmes of adjustment to automation and advanced technological change, which should be consulted by governments, employers and workers when introducing technical innovations,

Recognising that these problems vary in importance as between countries, industries, and occupations and that the solutions appropriate to each case will not necessarily be the same in industrialised and in developing countries,

Noting that the special employment and social conditions prevailing in developing countries were taken into consideration in the conclusions concerning the World Employment Programme which were adopted by the International Labour Conference at its 56th Session, and referring to information on the situation in developing countries presented in the Director-General's Report to the 57th Session of the International Labour Conference,

Considering that the following international labour Conventions and Recommendations, although not specifically focused on technological change, nevertheless provide important principles and programmes which can serve to meet some aspects of the social problems arising from modern technology:

- Social Security (Minimum Standards) Convention, 1952 (No. 102);
- Employment Policy Convention, 1964 (No. 122);
- Employment Service Recommendation, 1948 (No. 83);
- Vocational Guidance Recommendation, 1949 (No. 87);

- Reduction of Hours of Work Recommendation, 1962 (No. 116);
- Vocational Training Recommendation, 1962 (No. 117);
- Termination of Employment Recommendation, 1963 (No. 119);
- Employment Policy Recommendation, 1964 (No. 122);
- Communications within the Undertaking Recommendation, 1967 (No. 129);

Considering furthermore that no comprehensive international instrument has hitherto been adopted which provides recommendations for effective protection to workers affected by the social effects of technological change;

A. Declares that the following principles and programmes should guide governments, employers and workers and their organisations, in dealing with the labour and social implications of automation and other technological developments.

## I. Labour-management relations

1. Governments, employers and workers should consult and co-operate, in the framework of appropriate bipartite or tripartite bodies, at the various levels of the economy, in examining the impact of new technology and in devising programmes which offer the most effective protection to workers against harmful social effects of technological change where they occur.

2. Labour-management consultation and negotiations on the complex problems of technological change require co-operative attitudes and effective communication between the parties; sufficient time for investigation; and structures of employers' and workers' organisations and consultative and negotiating machinery capable of rapidly solving issues and implementing decisions.

3. Appropriate machinery and procedures for consultation and collective bargaining between employers and workers should be developed or created where existing institutions are not adequate, at the level of industry or of industrial branches or of the undertaking, or at all these levels and, in relation to multinational firms, following methods compatible with the usage and principles in force in each country.

4. An effective policy of communication should ensure that information is given and that consultation takes place between the parties concerned before decisions on matters of major interest are taken by management, in so far as disclosure of the information will not cause damage to either party. At the level of the undertaking, representatives of workers and of their organisations should be effectively associated with modernisation or reorganisation schemes.

## II. Full employment

5. Efforts to achieve and maintain full, productive and freely chosen employment–whether through planning, goal-setting or fiscal, monetary and manpower policies–are essential in order to provide a favourable economic climate for the satisfactory solution of displacement problems arising from the introduction of new technology.

6. When increases in productivity take place as the result of technological change, every effort should be made to ensure that economic growth is sufficient to

absorb to the greatest possible extent both the manpower made available by such productivity gains and any expected expansion of the labour force. In implementing full employment goals, technological change is only one of a complex of factors which make up the total economic situation.

7. Consideration should be given to the possible effects on placement of available labour of reductions in total work time through, for example, earlier retirement, longer paid vacations, additional holidays with pay and shorter daily and weekly work schedules, having regard to the specific economic, industrial and social conditions and practices in different countries.

8. In situations of widespread unemployment, as found particularly in developing countries, the employment effects of using advanced technology must be considered together with its role in economic development. Special consideration should be given to the development and utilisation of technology appropriate to the labour and capital resources of such countries, taking into account the need to meet international competition, particularly in export industries. Whenever a choice of technology is available, developing countries should seek to raise the level of employment by ensuring that capital-intensive technology is confined to uses in which it is clearly cheaper in real terms and more efficient.

## III. Preventing or minimising job loss

9. When introducing new technology, employers should undertake a maximum effort to ensure that there be no resultant loss in employment for any member of the work force. If it is unavoidable that some workers lose their employment, management has the responsibility to give workers and their representatives and, when appropriate, government manpower authorities, advance indication as soon as possible. If the subsequent consultation and negotiation among the parties is to be effective, the period of notice must allow sufficient time to decide upon and implement the necessary manpower adjustments.

10. Joint efforts to avoid redundancies should utilise the process of normal manpower reduction, supplemented by the use of temporary hiring and incentives to induce voluntary separations, to the maximum extent possible. Whenever feasible, the gradual phasing-in of new technology should be adapted to permit such processes to operate more effectively. To meet special manpower adjustment problems, it may prove useful to make special benefits available for early retirement on a voluntary basis.

11. To assist in the redistribution of the work force, detailed data should be maintained on the work experience and qualifications of employees, and such records should be open to inspection by the employee concerned or the workers' representative in the plant.

12. Workers who are transferred to other jobs within an undertaking following structural or technological changes should receive their former pay during any retraining period, subject to national practice. To the greatest extent possible, the new job should be equivalent, involving no loss in pay or promotion opportunities.

13. If the introduction of technological change results in the displacement of a worker and he is transferred to another plant of the same undertaking, then he should

be given certain fundamental assistance which should include, for example—

(a) provision for the reimbursement of reasonable expenses incurred where a change of residence is necessary;
(b) aid in ensuring the worker's assimilation and acceptance into the new community;
(c) assistance in solving the problem of housing;
(d) temporary allowance for additional costs at the new location either because of living away from the family, or the possible increase in the cost of daily travel to and from work;
(e) payment of an appropriate wage or salary and maintenance of acquired service benefits, so that the worker does not suffer a noticeable downgrading in his standard of living; and
(f) training as required, at the new location within the undertaking, without cost to the worker.

14. Where the reduction in the work force due to technological change is likely to be only temporary, the parties might consider the use of work-sharing arrangements, provided that the period envisaged in such arrangements is short. In such cases the workers should be compensated to an appropriate extent for their loss of earnings, either by the concern or by the public authorities.

15. Special efforts should be made to protect the jobs of older or disabled workers and other persons for whom re-employment is especially difficult.

16. Government also have responsibilities in regard to the prevention of job loss. Depending on the specific circumstances, these should include assistance to employers and unions in planning for technological change, legal protection for handicapped workers, and other manpower services.

## IV. Assistance for workers who lose their employment

17. Unemployment benefit and social security schemes or other benefit systems should provide a range of adequate benefits for workers affected by technological change. These should not necessarily be limited to providing daily cash allowances to replace total or partial loss of earnings but should also meet, during the period of readjustment, additional expenses in connection with retraining, change of residence, rehabilitation, etc. Entitlement to other social security benefits (medical care, family allowances, etc.) and the accrual of rights under old-age, disability and survivors' schemes should be maintained. The supplementary benefits for training or retraining should be designed so that the total of the benefits paid to workers during the training period is more than unemployment insurance benefits but less than the salary they might have expected to receive in their new employment. Where the economic situation does not permit the adoption of such income security measures, consideration should be given to measures of assistance and relief.

18. Governments should provide, in co-operation with employers' and workers' organisations, an employment service adequately organised and financed for the purpose of matching individual job applications and vacancies. In carrying out its work it should make efforts to collect and analyse data on current and prospective

supply and demand of the various occupational categories of labour, and such data should include information on employment opportunities and conditions of life and work in other areas.

19. Sufficient advance notice on the manpower effects of planned substantial technological changes should be supplied by employers to this service, and the workers concerned should be given every facility to avail themselves freely of its counsel and help in finding suitable alternative employment, including that involving a change of occupation or of residence.

20. The employment service, within the limits of its competence and in relation with the competent authorities, should make efforts to remove economic obstacles to geographical mobility by providing financial relocation assistance, and adequate housing and community facilities where there are job vacancies.

21. Training programmes, including selection and job counselling, should be established by the competent authorities for workers, in co-operation with the employment service and, if possible, with prospective employers. Such programmes should cover trades and occupations with good employment prospects. The main responsibility for retraining of workers to be transferred within the undertaking rests with the employer, but appropriate assistance should be provided by governments or other competent bodies.

## V. Preparation for new occupational requirements

22. Governments, employers and workers, and their organisations share responsibility for co-operating in the adaptation of the labour force to the rapidly changing skill requirements of modern technology, this co-operation being especially important with regard to all actions envisaged in this section.

23. In the light of these changes, governments should give serious consideration to the structure and content of their basic education system, the size and scope of their efforts in vocational guidance and training, and the adequacy of apprenticeship and other in-plant training schemes.

24. General education and training prior to entry into industry should be based on the concept of giving workers the greatest scope for advancement, of allowing them the greatest possible flexibility and of providing them with a wide range of interests to facilitate their psychological adaptation to modern production techniques. Technological change should also be used to grant adequate opportunity for promotion by pursuing sound policies of selection of workers for advancement and possible suitable training facilities.

25. Public authorities have the responsibility to provide vocational counselling in the framework of the public education system and employment services; to disseminate information required for training and education planning, including forecasts on the manpower impact of technological change; and to encourage and assist training schemes set up by employers, workers and their organisations and other competent bodies. Public authorities, in co-operation with employers' and workers' organisations, should set standards of training, subject to national practice.

26. With respect to in-school vocational training, which is a principal form of modern vocational training, the subjects taught, the teaching methods used and the

duration of the programmes should be geared to the needs of modern industry, due account being taken of the special situation existing in developing countries. The inclusion of fundamental theory in such courses and their organisation according to training units are two approaches which can assist students to adapt more easily to future skill changes and to pursue advanced technical studies.

27. In-plant training remains one of the most important methods of vocational training. Whether conducted entirely within industry or combined with classes of related instruction in educational institutions, as in the case of many apprenticeship systems, such training should be carefully and systematically planned to build logically upon a progression of skills and to adapt to changing technological requirements.

28. During the period of employment, workers should be provided with opportunities for further training with a view to providing them with career prospects up to their age of retirement, taking full account of the physical and mental requirements of different jobs and of the age and ability of the workers.

29. Technical advances also create adjustment problems for managerial and supervisory staff. Systematic training courses should be provided on a cyclical schedule, with government and employer support, to assist such personnel in keeping up to date on technical matters and their social impact and to provide guidance on management's role in initiating and introducing new technology, and on its increasing social responsibilities.

30. Further training should be made available to teaching personnel on a continuing basis to keep them abreast of teaching and technical developments. It is necessary that teachers of technical subjects periodically be given an opportunity to undertake practical work or to take part in courses, so as to keep up to date on recent technical developments and to keep in touch with the reality of industrial work. Industry should co-operate with governments in making such opportunities available to vocational teachers not actually employed in industry.

## VI. Health and safety and some other conditions of work

31. One objective of the use of modern technology should be an improvement of the safety and health of workers. To deal with those aspects of technical change which may be harmful to safety and health, the following measures are recommended:

(a) testing of new technological equipment by a competent service or body where it is necessary to evaluate potential risks;

(b) periodic revisions of safety and health regulations and inspection systems in order to adapt them to the conditions of technological change;

(c) providing detailed instruction on the use of new machinery or methods to affected workers when technological changes are introduced, or if possible prior to such introduction, in order to avoid endangering the health or safety of the operators and their fellow workers;

(d) including safety and health issues arising from technical change in the curriculum of vocational training courses.

32. The rising costs of modern machinery and the spread of continuous processes may lead to an increasing use of shift work; any disadvantages should be

limited whenever possible. Determination of an appropriate compensation for shift work and of methods to share its burden equitably are matters for collective bargaining, or other methods of negotiation according to national practice. The importance of shift rotation, where possible, should be carefully considered.

33. When necessary to compensate for special strain resulting from new technology, consideration should be given to reduced hours (for example, more frequent breaks or a shortened workday) with no loss in pay. Modern technology should lead, among other advantages, to a gradual reduction of hours of work to the extent that economic conditions permit.

34. The characteristics of the new jobs are likely to involve shifts in the importance of such job evaluation factors as responsibility for equipment, skill, initiative, working conditions and attentiveness. To the extent that this takes place, job evaluation plans will have to be reviewed and adjusted to account for these factors. If this process results in a downgrading for any jobs, workers performing those jobs should not suffer a reduction from their previous wage level as long as they remain in the job. The setting of the wages for new jobs should be the subject of negotiation in accordance with appropriate methods.

35. It should be an accepted principle to give all employees of the undertaking a fair share of the benefits resulting from the increased productivity which accompanies technological change. The extent to which benefits resulting from the increased productivity which accompanies technological change accrue to the plant's employees should be the subject of negotiations, bearing in mind the conditions prevailing in the economy and governmental policies.

B. Calls on member States who have not yet done so to consider urgently the ratification of the Conventions and the application of the Recommendations listed in the preamble of this resolution.

C. Urges governments, together with employers' and workers' organisations, to adopt and implement, by legislative action or otherwise according to national custom and practice, programmes to implement the principles and programmes set forth in the preceding section A.

D. Invites the Governing Body of the International Labour Office to request the Director-General—

*(a)* to carry out studies on the social problems of technological development, in so far as possible with other international organisations, in particular with regard to—
  (i) development trends, especially the scale and rate of technological change;
  (ii) the probable demand for labour in specific areas and industries;
  (iii) over-all studies on the kind of action taken in this field in countries having comparable socio-economic systems, and on the way such action works;
  (iv) the development of internationally comparable occupational descriptions in key occupations;
  (v) use which the developing countries might make of the experience acquired in the industrialised world; and
  (vi) the evolution of new types of technology suitable to the special needs and conditions of developing countries;

*(b)* to provide developing countries, at their request, with suitable technical and research assistance to ensure that the introduction of technological innovation is accomplished with positive results and not accompanied by social disadvantages;

*(c)* to include the social problems of technological development and the ways and means whereby such problems might be solved in the training programmes of the ILO and associated institutions; and

*(d)* to include the social problems of technological development in the agenda of future sessions of Industrial Committees and regional conferences.

E. Requests the Governing Body, in the light of the conclusions of this session of the conference, to put the question of the social effects of technological change on the agenda of a future session of the International Labour Conference, with a view to the adoption of international instruments.

57th Session, 1972

## 3. Development of the ILO's programme for the improvement of industrial relations

The General Conference of the International Labour Organisation,

Reaffirming the solemn obligation of the ILO, as contained in the Declaration of Philadelphia, to "further among nations of the world programmes which will achieve: *(a)* full employment and the raising of standards of living;... *(e)* the effective recognition of the right of collective bargaining, the co-operation of management and labour in the continuous improvement of productive efficiency and the collaboration of workers and employers in the preparation and application of social and economic measures",

Considering that the World Employment Programme (WEP) and its central objectives of implementing the Declaration of Principles and Programme of Action of the World Employment Conference provide well-defined objectives for ILO action in the future,

Considering that the International Programme for the Improvement of Working Conditions and Environment (PIACT), with its essential task of improving conditions of work and life and promoting occupational health and safety, likewise provides clear guidelines for future ILO activity,

Considering further that the existence of an effective system of industrial relations in each country is an indispensable instrument for reconciling different and often divergent interests, thereby creating conditions for increased productivity and improvement of working conditions and for full employment and economic and social justice,

Recognising that the aim of establishing and maintaining sound industrial relations is clearly within the competence of and is a long-standing mandate of the ILO,

Asserting that the participation of the three constituent groups of the ILO—viz. governments and employers' and workers' organisations—is an essential factor in drawing up effective programmes relating to the development and utilisation of human resources whose ultimate objective is human fulfilment,

Recognising that the existence of fully effective organisations representing employers and workers is a prerequisite of tripartism in each country and recognising also that this should be an important objective in major programmes of industrial relations of the ILO,

Noting, therefore, that there is a need for the ILO to develop its programme for the improvement of industrial relations,

Noting, with approval, that the Governing Body of the International Labour Office has placed on the agenda of the 66th (1980) Session of the International Labour Conference an item on the promotion of collective bargaining;

1. Invites the Governing Body of the International Labour Office to instruct the Director-General to develop its programme for the improvement of industrial relations the principal aims of which will be—

(a) to ensure the growth of representative, free and independent national workers' and employers' organisations in accordance with the Freedom of Association and Protection of the Right to Organise Convention, 1948 (No. 87), and the Right to Organise and Collective Bargaining Convention, 1949 (No. 98), the Rural Workers' Organisations Convention, 1975 (No. 141), and the Labour Relations (Public Service) Convention, 1978 (No. 151);

(b) to promote institutional structures which will enable employers' and workers' organisations to play an effective role in the establishment and implementation of development plans, for instance through tripartite committees specifically constituted for such purposes;

(c) to promote sound industrial relations systems, taking into account conditions prevailing in each country and in which the protection provided in the Workers' Representatives Convention, 1971 (No. 135), is fully assured;

(d) to strengthen ILO operational activities through training courses, seminars, workshops and study tours to improve labour management relations, and meetings with a view to an exchange of views and experience on the role of employers' and workers' organisations in the development process;

(e) to assist member States and employers' and workers' organisations according to their needs in the development of tripartite institutions and procedures in line with the Tripartite Consultation (International Labour Standards) Convention, 1976 (No. 144), and the Tripartite Consultation (Activities of the International Labour Organisation) Recommendation, 1976 (No. 152);

(f) to implement fully the International Programme for the Improvement of Working Conditions and Environment (PIACT) and the World Employment Programme (WEP) as set out in the Declaration of Principles and Programme of Action of the World Employment Conference.

2. Calls upon governments and employers' and workers' organisations to co-operate fully in the development and implementation of such a comprehensive programme.

65th Session, 1979

# B. Resolution of the Preparatory Technical Maritime Conference

## 1. Industrial relations in the shipping industry

The Preparatory Technical Maritime Conference,

Having met in Geneva from 13 to 24 October 1975,

Having examined the question of industrial relations, which is the first item on its agenda, and

Having noted that the Freedom of Association and Protection of the Right to Organise Convention, 1948, and the Right to Organise and Collective Bargaining Convention, 1949, which are applicable to the shipping industry, have been ratified by many, though not by all, maritime countries, and

Having noted the terms of other international labour Conventions and Recommendations which are concerned with industrial relations and are general in their scope, in particular the Collective Agreements Recommendation, 1951, the Voluntary Conciliation and Arbitration Recommendation, 1951, the Co-operation at the Level of the Undertaking Recommendation, 1952, the Consultation (Industrial and National Levels) Recommendation, 1960, the Termination of Employment Recommendation, 1963, the Communications within the Undertaking Recommendation, 1967, the Examination of Grievances Recommendation, 1967, and the Workers' Representatives Convention and Recommendation, 1971, and

Considering that agreed approaches to the full and effective implementation in the shipping industry of the principles embodied in these instruments, where applicable, are desirable;

Adopts the following resolution and requests the Governing Body to transmit it to governments and to shipowners' and seafarers' organisations:

1. (1) The existence of strong and independent organisations of shipowners and seafarers, able to represent, further and defend the interests of their members, to enter into negotiations and to ensure the application and observance of agreements arrived at, should be recognised by all concerned in accordance with national law and practice as being an important factor in the solution of the complex problems of the shipping industry and in its adaptation to technological change.

(2) In accordance with the above, shipowners' and seafarers' organisations should recognise each other not only for purposes of bargaining and the conclusion of collective agreements on wages and conditions of employment but as parties with a mutual interest in the promotion of the industry and the protection of those deriving their livelihood from it.

2. There should be close consultation and co-operation between shipowners and seafarers and their various organisations on all matters of mutual concern.

Account should be taken, in this connection, of provisions of international labour Conventions and Recommendations specifically calling for such consultation and cooperation on particular issues, such as Paragraph 4 of the Employment of Seafarers (Technical Developments) Recommendation, 1970.

3. Representative organisations of shipowners and seafarers should work actively together in the establishment and implementation of policies and programmes for the benefit of seafarers and of the shipping industry, for instance in the framework of the joint accident prevention committees envisaged in the Prevention of Accidents (Seafarers) Convention, 1970, of the welfare boards envisaged in the Seafarers' Welfare Recommendation, 1970, and in joint training programmes.

4. There should be machinery appropriate to national conditions which permits, preferably on a voluntary basis, the prompt settlement of disputes between shipowners and seafarers through conciliation, mediation or arbitration, in a climate of mutual confidence.

5. (1) There should be appropriate arrangements for training, in modern methods and sound practices, of those persons who are responsible for personnel management and industrial relations both in shipping undertakings as a whole and on board individual ships.

(2) Representatives of seafarers within shipping undertakings and on board ship should have appropriate opportunities for education and training in industrial relations practices and for receiving information concerning issues confronting the industry. Account should be taken in this connection of the Paid Educational Leave Recommendation, 1974.

6. All parties concerned should seek to maintain good industrial relations on board ship. Importance should be attached in this connection—

*(a)* to modern concepts of personnel management and sound labour management techniques, reviewing, as necessary, methods of maintaining discipline on board, with a view of finding acceptable alternatives to existing legislation;

*(b)* to effective communication between the shipowner and master, the master and the seafarer, and between the seafarers and their organisations, in particular by the rapid dissemination and exchange of complete and relevant information;

*(c)* to the prompt settlement of grievances, in accordance with the Examination of Grievances Recommendation, 1967;

*(d)* to arrangements, in accordance with national law or practice or by collective agreement, whereby seafarers may select or elect one or more of their colleagues as appropriate to act as their representative(s) on board.

Preparatory Technical Maritime Conference, 1975

# C. Resolutions and conclusions adopted by the ILO Regional Conferences

## Freedom of association and labour relations

### 1. International labour standards in Asia, in particular those relating to human rights and trade union freedoms

The Eighth Asian Regional Conference of the International Labour Organisation,

Meeting in Colombo from 30 September to 9 October 1975,

Considering that international labour standards, and especially those relating to fundamental human rights and the full exercise of freedom of association, have been and continue to be of vital importance for the attainment of the ILO's objectives,

Recognising the function of ILO standards in ensuring that national plans and policies give due attention to the improving of living and working conditions both as a contributing factor to and as the ultimate purpose of economic development,

Considering the urgent need for women to be ensured full equality of opportunity and rights with men,

Recalling the conclusion reached by the Seventh Asian Regional Conference that "the position of Asian countries with regard to the ratification and application of Conventions is capable of substantial improvement" and that some of the existing difficulties "could be overcome by governments genuinely desiring to do so",

Noting with concern that many member States in the Asian region have not yet ratified the Freedom of Association and Protection of the Right to Organise Convention, 1948 (No. 87), the Right to Organise and Collective Bargaining Convention, 1949 (No. 98), and the Workers' Representatives Convention, 1971 (No. 135), which lay down the minimum standards of freedom of association, and that the average number of ratifications by the countries of the Asian region continues to be significantly lower than in other regions of the world,

Considering the useful role which can be played by tripartite consultative machinery in systematically examining all questions relating to the ratification and application of ILO instruments,

Considering the need for further measures to ensure full understanding of the obligations in respect to international labour standards and to facilitate the implementation of these obligations,

Noting the positive results which have been obtained, particularly in other regions of the world, from recourse to the procedure of direct contacts between governments and the ILO in facilitating the fulfilment of obligations in respect of international labour standards and recalling the recommendations made by the Asian Advisory Committee and the Seventh Asian Regional Conference regarding use of this procedure by Asian countries,

Recalling the resolutions concerning freedom of association for employers' and workers' organisations and their role in social and economic development and concerning promotion of rural workers' and peasant organisations in Asia, adopted by the Seventh Asian Regional Conference,

Noting the adoption of the Rural Workers' Organisations Convention (No. 141) and Recommendation (No. 149), 1975,

Noting that the International Labour Conference will have before it in 1976, for adoption, instruments relating to the establishment of tripartite machinery at the national level to promote the implementation of international labour standards,

Emphasising once again the leading role that the International Labour Organisation has played and must continue to play in defending, widening and safeguarding trade union freedoms in the world;

1. Reaffirms the universal validity of the principles of freedom of association and calls on all ILO member States in the Asian region to establish tripartite consultative machinery in which the representatives of governments, employers and workers can regularly and systematically review national law and practice in the light of ILO standards with a view to advising governments on the measures to be taken for the ratification of further Conventions and for the implementation of international labour standards.

2. Strongly urges member States in the Asian region which have not done so to ratify and apply the Right of Association (Agriculture) Convention, 1921 (No. 11), the Freedom of Association and Protection of the Right to Organise Convention, 1948 (No. 87), and the Right to Organise and Collective Bargaining Convention, 1949 (No. 98), the Workers' Representatives Convention, 1971 (No. 135), and the Rural Workers' Organisations Convention, 1975 (No. 141), and, pending ratification, to guarantee strict observance of the principles set forth in these Conventions.

3. Appeals to member States in the Asian region to respect the principles embodied in these Conventions when adopting their national laws and regulations and when participating in any regional economic consultation.

4. Emphasises the special importance for the balanced social and economic development of Asian countries of the ratification and implementation not only of the above-mentioned Conventions relating to freedom of association, but also of Conventions in the following fields—

*(a)* equality of opportunity and treatment: Discrimination (Employment and Occupation) Convention, 1958 (No. 111), and Equal Remuneration Convention, 1951 (No. 100);

*(b)* freedom of labour: Forced Labour Convention, 1930 (No. 29), and Abolition of Forced Labour Convention, 1957 (No. 105);

*(c)* promotion of employment; Employment Policy Convention, 1964 (No. 122);

*(d)* minimum wages and the protection of wages: Minimum Wage Fixing Convention, 1970 (No. 131), and Protection of Wages Convention, 1949 (No. 95);

*(e)* minimum age for employment: Minimum Age Convention, 1973 (No. 138);

*(f)* labour inspection: Labour Inspection Convention, 1947 (No. 81), and Labour Inspection (Agriculture) Convention, 1969 (No. 129);

*(g)* social security, including adequate protection in respect of employment injuries: Social Security (Minimum Standards) Convention, 1952 (No. 102), and Employment Injury Benefits Convention, 1964 (No. 121).

5. Calls upon the Governing Body of the International Labour Office to pursue measures for the review and revision of the Plantations Convention, 1958 (No. 110), so as to adapt the provisions relating to the scope of this Convention to the realities and needs of Asian countries.

6. Invites the Governing Body of the International Labour Office to instruct the Director-General to convene as a matter of urgency a tripartite meeting to discuss the ILO's fact-finding studies on multinational enterprises, as well as future ILO action in this field, with particular reference to freedom of association.

7. Further invites the Governing Body of the International Labour Office to instruct the Director-General to draw up and implement a coherent programme designed to promote the protection, strengthening and expansion of trade union rights, including the right to collective bargaining, in the undertaking, in the economy and in society, in particular by preparing reports with a view to the adoption of new international standards for the protection of human rights and trade union freedoms, in accordance with the resolution concerning trade union rights and their relation to civil liberties, adopted by the International Labour Conference at its 54th (1970) Session.

8. Calls upon the International Labour Office to ensure that technical co-operation programmes lead to a wider implementation of ILO standards.

9. Invites Asian governments to strengthen the services within their ministries of labour responsible for relations with the ILO, so that they may be better equipped to deal with questions relating to international labour standards.

10. Recommends Asian States which encounter legal or practical difficulties in ensuring the application of ratified Conventions, or in resolving other problems which may arise in respect of international labour standards, to have recourse to the procedure of direct contacts with the ILO and, where appropriate, also to have recourse to technical cooperation to overcome such difficulties.

11. Requests the International Labour Office to intensify action aimed at helping countries in Asia to draw fully upon ILO standards in the development of their social policies and legislation by such means as—

*(a)* the organisation of further regional seminars on international labour standards for government officials and trade unionists, as well as for employers, if they should so desire;

*(b)* short missions by ILO officials to advise governments, employers and workers on questions relating to Conventions and Recommendations and their implementation;

*(c)* fellowships to government officials and trade union and employer officers to study questions relating to standards at the Organisation's headquarters in Geneva, particularly in connection with their attendance at the International Labour Conference or other meetings.

12. Calls upon the Governing Body of the International Labour Office to ensure that the problems encountered in the ratification and implementation of international labour Conventions in Asia continue to be the subject of comprehensive reviews, carried out in consultation with governments and employers' and workers' organisations, and be considered as a separate agenda item at the next session of the Asian Advisory Committee and at the next Asian Regional Conference.

13. Expresses the wish that the next Asian Advisory committee will, in the light of the above-mentioned reports, give consideration to the desirability of placing on the agenda of the Ninth Asian Regional Conference of the International Labour Organisation an item concerning the protection of human rights and trade union freedoms in the undertaking, in the economy and in society in Asia.

Resolution of the 8th Asian Regional Conference, Colombo, 1975

## 2. Freedom of association, labour relations and development in Asia

### General principles

1. In their search for new and effective approaches to national development, most Asian countries are at present engaged in the reconsideration and revision of their labour relations systems. The relevance of labour relations to development is, in fact, increasingly recognised. A constructive relationship between workers and employers, between workers' organisations and employers' organisations, and between these organisations and the public authorities is of fundamental importance for the formulation and implementation of development policies, the organisation of the production process at the plant and industry levels and the equitable distribution of income. On the other hand, the absence of constructive relations between the three parties may jeopardise efforts aimed at the promotion of social and economic development.

2. Progress in national development efforts depends on the support of workers' and employers' organisations, which again is dependent on their effective participation in the labour relations system. A prerequisite of such participation is the establishment and expansion of strong, representative and independent organisations based on the respect of the principles of freedom of association. Governments should therefore give serious consideration to the ratification and effective implementation of ILO Conventions on freedom of association. The existence of restrictions on the rights of workers' and employers' organisations is likely to constitute a serious obstacle to the adoption by workers and employers and their organisations of a constructive attitude towards the development efforts of the governments. Such an attitude is a fundamental element in any labour relations system and should be geared to the shaping of an agreed approach to development policies and their implementation.

3. The adjustment of labour relations patterns to development requirements should not impinge on freedom of association, the right to organise and the right to bargain collectively. Within the framework of this general principle, each country is expected to develop its own system of labour relations, which will have to strike the optimum balance between apparently diverging needs arising in the process of development, such as in the areas of employment creation and a fairer income distribution. The best way of achieving this is by effective communication, bipartite and tripartite negotiation and consultation between trade unions, employers' organisations and the government, at various levels, and through effective dispute settlement procedures, in particular conciliation and arbitration procedures. Arbitration procedures should not only be impartial and independent but should also be

established in such a manner as to ensure the confidence of the parties involved. National labour relations policy may include voluntary guidelines for the promotion of constructive relations between workers' and employers' organisations and the government, agreed upon between the parties, and which would take into account the particular social and economic conditions prevailing in each country, the patterns of behaviour and the cultural traditions.

## Role of the ILO

4. In the efforts of Asian governments, employers' organisations and workers' organisations to work out systems of labour relations which are conducive to national development and which respect freedom of association, the ILO has a major role to play. While it is recognised that the policy decisions on the orientation and content of labour relations policy should be left to joint deliberations between the government and the employers' and workers' organisations of each country of Asia and the Pacific, taking into account the specific conditions and circumstances of each country, the ILO can assist in these efforts in a number of ways.

5. In a general way, the ILO should step up its activities in the Asian and Pacific region in the field of freedom of association, labour relations and development and should allocate a larger portion of its resources to this work. It should, in particular, strengthen its regional staff by people who have specialised knowledge and experience with labour relations in the region, particularly as regards labour-management relations at the enterprise level.

6. In pursuing and strengthening its work on the linkages between labour relations and development, the ILO should be guided by the general principles and considerations set out in the first section of these conclusions. In particular, the ILO's future work should concentrate on the following:

### Studies

7. The ILO should develop a programme of studies on the labour relations situation in Asia and the Pacific. Such studies, rather than being academic and theoretical in nature, and rather than describing the labour relations legislation of the various countries, should take the form of factual surveys.

8. In order to ensure that these studies are as close as possible to the reality and reflect the views of those directly involved in the labour relations processes, it is indispensable that ILO studies be carried out in close association with the governments and employers' and workers' organisations concerned.

9. It is of great importance that the ILO, in carrying out these studies, make full use of research and other suitable institutions which exist in the region and which have experience in carrying out labour relations surveys. At the same time, the ILO should assist in creating such institutions and should help those already in existence.

10. A strong emphasis should be placed on enterprise surveys both in the public and private sectors. The purpose of such surveys should be to detect and analyse the practical problems arising on a day-to-day basis between employers and workers and their representatives at the enterprise and shop floor level. In carrying

out such surveys, the ILO should select, in consultation with the government and employers' and workers' organisations concerned, enterprises which are typical of the situation in the country concerned and not necessarily those which have been particularly successful in setting up labour relations systems based on co-operation between employers and workers. It is important that the ILO studies should be based on discussions with the management and workers in the enterprises concerned.

11. Another area in which the ILO should undertake studies and surveys is collective bargaining and other forms of workers' involvement in decision making at the enterprise and industry level. Here again, emphasis should be placed on what happens in actual fact around bargaining tables or in joint consultation meetings. Such studies should also aim at identifying possible areas of co-operation between management and labour, including forms of and prerequisites for such co-operation.

12. The ILO should also carry out surveys of the way in which conciliation and arbitration bodies function in various countries of the region. The subject of such studies and surveys should be the day-to-day work of individual conciliators, conciliation boards and arbitration bodies, courts and tribunals and industrial relations commissions.

13. In all its studies on these and other aspects of labour relations in the region, the ILO should place particular emphasis on the need to identify the factors which foster as well as those which hamper the development of constructive labour relations, conducive to development.

14. The surveys and studies to be undertaken by the ILO should take account of the specific social, economic and cultural factors of the countries concerned. The studies therefore need to be backed up by analytical research into these various factors which aims at explaining the "why" of various labour relations phenomena in Asian countries by placing the employer-employee relationship within the social and cultural context of Asia and the Pacific. It is expected that such studies will thus re-examine the functioning within the context of each country of the region, and of such labour relations practices as collective bargaining, labour-management consultation, conciliation, arbitration or workers' participation.

15. It is important that governments, employers' organisations and workers' organisations should not only be associated—as stressed above—with the preparation and carrying out of such studies but that the outcome and results of such studies should be discussed with those directly concerned. The aim of the studies and research should be to promote endeavours to improve labour relations and to assist the parties concerned in better understanding and appreciating the problems in their mutual relationships so that they can jointly try to work out solutions.

*Training and promotion of exchanges of views*

16. Another important means of action by which the ILO can contribute to the promotion of sound labour relations in Asia and the Pacific is training. In a general way, the ILO should broaden and intensify its training activities for trade unionists, officials of employers' organisations, management representatives in charge of personnel and labour relations matters and government officials who are particularly concerned with the relationships between employers and workers.

17. Such training activities should be conducted through seminars, training courses, workshops and other meetings through the medium of the languages spoken in the region. While it is very important that there should be separate training activities for government, employers' and workers' representatives, including women, it is equally important to arrange for training courses and seminars in which representatives of different interest groups can be brought together so that they can better understand and appreciate the views and aspirations of the other parties. The ILO should, for instance, organise training courses in which it would bring together managers, trade unionists and government industrial relations officers, or shop stewards, line managers and personnel managers, or—more specifically—employers' and workers' representatives in collective bargaining or joint consultation from the same enterprise or industry. The ILO should also extend its training activities in the labour relations field to those who are not directly involved in labour relations but whose role in their countries has a direct bearing on labour relations, such as officials of ministries of industry, finance, economic affairs and the planning agencies, in order to make them better aware of the importance and complexities of labour relations issues.

18. One form of training, to which the ILO should pay particular attention, is the organisation of study tours. Here again study tours should be organised separately and jointly for representatives of trade unions, employers' organisations and governments. While such study tours should primarily provide an opportunity for the participants to become acquainted with the labour relations situation in other countries of the Asian and Pacific region, such study tours should also be organised for participants from the region to other parts of the world so that they can compare their experience with that of countries outside the Asian and Pacific region.

19. Another way by which the ILO could contribute to the improvement of mutual understanding among governments, employers and trade unions is the convening of tripartite meetings in order to facilitate an exchange of views among them on various topical issues of labour relations. Such tripartite meetings should be organised on a regional, subregional or national level. More specifically, the ILO could contribute to the promotion of sound labour relations policies by helping to convene national meetings of labour policy makers in governments, and high-level trade union and employers' representatives, to discuss changes in the country's labour relations policy or industrial relations legislation, whenever such changes are envisaged and the government concerned wishes to hold such meetings for exchanges of views with the help and participation of the ILO or under ILO auspices.

20. In certain Asian and Pacific countries it might be possible to extend, at the request of a particular government, the facilities of the ILO so as to become more directly involved with the promotion of sound labour relations. In a country which might be interested in such an effort and, subject to the agreement of the government as well as of the employers' and workers' organisations concerned, a tripartite—or sometimes perhaps bipartite—meeting could be convened at the economy-wide level or at the level of a particular industry with the technical and moral support and participation of the ILO. At such meetings the ILO would not only provide technical information and serve as a catalyst for the testing of ideas but could, if the parties so request, actively assist in bringing about, with the help of its technical experience and competence, some form of arrangement in which labour relations are linked with

national development. Such arrangement could take the form of a code of labour relations practices, basic agreement, agreed guidelines for the conduct of sound labour relations or some other form of mutual co-operation. It would have to be understood that the responsibility for the development and implementation of such arrangement would be with the government and employers' and workers' organisations concerned. The role of the ILO would take the form of assistance, promotion, encouragement and technical servicing. It is understood that the ILO contribution to such an effort would be in conformity with the general principles developed by the Organisation.

Conclusions of the 9th Asian Regional Conference, Manila, 1980

## 3. Labour relations and development in the Americas

### I. The role and place of labour relations in the development process

1. Labour relations systems are closely related to the economic and social development process. A sound labour relations system which can promote consensus between the social partners as well as between them and the public authorities can reinforce industrial peace and reduce the number of labour disputes. This is essential for a successful development strategy based upon increased production and productivity. On the other hand, a labour relations system in which conflict prevails over consensus can destabilise economic and social relationships and thus block development efforts.

2. In Latin America and the Caribbean, labour relations systems frequently cover a limited percentage of the labour force. None the less, this coverage always includes the modern sector of the economy which many States in the region consider the key sector in their development strategy. Consequently, a sound labour relations system is an essential condition for ensuring that this key sector can make the development contribution expected of it.

### II. The content of a sound labour relations system and the development process

3. It is for each country to establish its own labour relations system in accordance with its own socio-economic framework, history, tradition and cultural values. And clearly the various labour relations systems in force in the region reflect these differences. Despite these differences, and whatever the social, political, cultural and economic context, the Conference considers that certain basic principles are indispensable elements of all sound labour relations systems in the region. Amongst these principles, special mention must be made of freedom of association and collective bargaining as set forth in the Freedom of Association and Protection of the Right to Organise Convention, 1948 (No. 87), and the Right to Organise and Collective Bargaining Convention, 1949 (No. 98). These basic principles of freedom

of association should be recognised by all governments in the region and be accompanied by appropriate guarantees against trade union discrimination. Workers' representatives in the undertaking should enjoy the protection and facilities afforded by the Workers' Representatives Convention, 1971 (No. 135) and Recommendation, 1971 (No. 143).

*Freedom of association*

4. Employers and workers should be free to establish organisations to represent their interests and to play an active role in the development process. In conformity with the principles expressed in Convention No. 87, it is for the workers and employers directly concerned to choose the type of organisation and the organisational structure which they consider best for defending their rights. Legislation should respect this free choice.

5. Since one of the aims of development is the promotion of and respect for human rights, including those basic liberties such as freedom of association for employers and workers, any restrictions on this freedom, in countries in the region where they still exist, should be eliminated by the member States concerned.

6. So as to preserve their identity and equal weight in the process of social dialogue, employers' and workers' organisations should be independent from each other and of the public authorities.

7. When employers' or workers' organisations establish relations with a political party or undertake political action to advance their economic and social objectives, these relations or this action should not be such as to transform these organisations into instruments of political parties or of the government.

*Collective bargaining*

8. The countries in the region should guarantee the social partners the right to determine employment conditions and their mutual relations through collective bargaining. The social partners should be able to bargain on all matters they consider appropriate. They should be able to bargain at the level they consider most appropriate in accordance with national practice.

9. Without prejudicing collective bargaining, the public authorities should ensure, through labour legislation, minimum labour conditions.

10. The State should encourage collective bargaining between the social partners by providing an appropriate framework to facilitate bargaining. Measures to promote collective bargaining should be guided by the principles contained in the Collective Bargaining Convention (No. 154) and Recommendation (No. 163) of 1981.

*Settlement of labour disputes*

11. As labour disputes can have a negative impact on the production process and hence on development, the State should make available suitable dispute settlement machinery, it being understood that the parties should have the opportunity in the first instance to resolve their conflicts without third-party intervention.

12. Procedures for the settlement of labour disputes should in no way undermine the rights of trade unions and employers' organisations.

13. Labour disputes in essential services should be settled through negotiation or, if not possible, by procedures such as mediation, conciliation and arbitration which offer guarantees of independence, impartiality and speediness and in which the parties can take part at every stage. Moreover, the term "essential services" should be as precisely and narrowly defined as possible, in accordance with national law and practice.

*Labour relations in public administration*

14. The Conference recalls that Convention No. 87 guarantees the right of employees in the public service to organise. The Conference calls upon the countries in the region where it is not yet recognised to extend this right to public servants. As provided for in the Labour Relations (Public Service) Convention, 1978 (No. 151), organisations of public employees should enjoy the right to negotiate, or to otherwise participate in the determination of, conditions of employment in the public service. Labour disputes in the public service should be settled through negotiations or, if this is not feasible, by conciliation, mediation or arbitration which ensure impartiality and which enjoy the trust of the parties. Those States of the region which have not ratified Convention No. 151 should consider the possibility of doing so.

*Labour relations in agriculture*

15. Labour relations in the rural sector should be based on the general principles mentioned in paragraph 4 of these conclusions. The States of the region should ratify and apply the Rural Workers' Organisations Convention, 1975 (No. 141).

*Workers' participation in the enterprise*

16. With due regard to national conditions, every effort should be made to develop methods of participation at the enterprise level which can contribute to the improvement of relations between employers and workers.

17. These methods should be determined by common agreement between the social partners and should not affect the collective bargaining process for the autonomy of the parties concerned.

18. Among these methods of participation, efforts should be made to encourage consultation and communication within the enterprise. Such methods may draw upon the principles contained in the Co-operation at the Level of the Undertaking Recommendation, 1952 (No. 94), and in the Communications within the Undertaking Recommendation, 1967 (No. 129).

## III. Concerted action and development

19. The Conference considers that, under certain conditions, concerted action between the social partners and the public authorities can be an appropriate means of

contributing to the formulation of economic and social policies at the national level. In particular, its usefulness is recognised in the present-day context in which, in view of the economic crisis, many countries in the region are obliged to adopt policies which call for sacrifice. Such policies could be better prepared and more acceptable if they were the outcome of consensus. In times of economic prosperity also, concerted action is an approach which can help to ensure a fairer distribution of benefits amongst all concerned.

20. Concerted action is viable only if certain conditions are fulfilled. One is that it should be the result of consultations or negotiations between the public authorities and independent and truly representative workers' and employers' organisations. Another condition is the recognition that concerted action is a process in which all parties can be called upon to make concessions and sacrifices and abide by agreements made. Finally, genuine concerted action should be voluntarily entered into.

21. The Conference considers that, despite practical problems involved in achieving genuine concerted action, efforts in this direction already undertaken by States in the region should be continued and encouraged. The Conference recalls that consultation and collaboration between the public authorities and organisations of employers and workers is one means of promoting concerted action and, in this connection, reaffirms the importance of the principles contained in the Consultation (Industrial and National Levels) Recommendation, 1960 (No. 113).

22. Neither the independence of employers' and workers' organisations nor the integrity of free collective bargaining should be jeopardised by concerted action.

## IV. ILO action

23. In the setting up and promotion of sound labour relations systems capable of playing a positive role in the establishment and implementation of development strategies, the expertise of the ILO could be availed of, in particular, as regards the following activities:

(a) the International Labour Office should promote the application of ILO standards and principles on labour relations;
(b) the ILO should encourage exchanges of views and opinions and the dissemination of information through tripartite technical meetings and seminars at the national and regional levels;
(c) ILO study missions might visit certain countries in the region, on the invitation of the government concerned, in order to examine the labour relations situation and, in appropriate cases, advise such governments as well as the social partners as to which aspects of such relations could be improved;
(d) ILO training programmes in labour relations, collective bargaining and dispute settlement should be continued and strengthened. Such programmes could be organised on a tripartite basis, as well as separately, for labour administration officials or the social partners. These programmes could be held in conjunction with the Inter-American Centre for Labour Administration, with the workers' education programme or that for employers' activities.

24. The ILO should assist States of the region to formulate a national labour relations policy, with the co-operation of the national employers' and workers'

organisations. Such policies might take the form of voluntary codes, declarations or basic agreements concluded by employers' and workers' organisations or adopted by tripartite bodies for consultation and cooperation. These codes, declarations or agreements could deal with such matters as mutual recognition of the social partners, collective bargaining and dispute settlement, and the promotion of co-operation within enterprises in various branches of the economy and at the national level.

Conclusions of the 12th Conference of American States Members of the ILO, Montreal, 1986

## Tripartism

### 1. Strengthening and furthering of tripartite co-operation

The Tenth Conference of American States Members of the International Labour Organisation, having met in Mexico City from 26 November to 5 December 1974,

Convinced of the value of the principles of tripartite co-operation and of the need to strengthen their application in the region,

Understanding that tripartism should operate within the evolution of each society as a dynamic element and as an element of co-operation, guaranteeing full freedom of association and independence of the three different sectors which are involved in the tripartite process and which form a part of each society,

Persuaded that it is necessary to enlarge the basis of such co-operation and promote tripartism in the fields of labour and social policy,

Considering that the observance of the principle of freedom of association and the strengthening of the representative bodies are basic to the full development of countries,

Noting the provisions of various Conventions, Recommendations and resolutions adopted by the ILO which enunciate the relevant principles of tripartite co-operation,

Noting further the relevant conclusions adopted by the Fourth Session of the Inter-American Advisory Committee, held in Lima in September 1973,

Recommends the governments of the region:

(a) to establish, at the national and regional level, tripartite bodies in keeping with the degree of economic and social development and the political and cultural circumstances of each country;

(b) to follow, in establishing such bodies, flexible criteria that take into account the interests of the parties and the institutional framework of each country and to seek to adjust to the greatest possible extent the general scope of action of such bodies, as well as the powers with which they are vested, to the particular conditions of each country;

(c) to secure in the composition and structure of such bodies all due respect for the principles of equity and equality of treatment and for the autonomy of each group;

(d) to adopt adequate standards for the regular, expeditious and effective functioning of tripartite bodies;

(e) to ensure that the powers of such bodies bear a close relationship to the range and subject-matter for which they were established; and, in the case of bodies with general competence, to impart to their operations a consultative and informative role oriented towards social change, without thereby excluding the possibility of specialised bodies or bodies concerned with specific matters being endowed with the necessary powers to fulfil their tasks;

(f) in order to give real meaning to tripartite bodies, to facilitate the strengthening of the participating organisations and, in particular, to guarantee full freedom of association, as defined in Convention No. 87, which provides that workers have the freedom to establish and to join trade union organisations of their own choosing;

(g) to consider the strengthening of labour administrations and, in particular, labour ministries as an essential factor in the promotion and development of tripartite co-operation;

(h) to ensure that the rights and independence of employers' organisations be fully respected so that they may participate effectively in the work of tripartite co-operation;

(i) to ensure, in determining the objectives and nature of tripartite co-operation bodies, that they do not replace representative bodies of the nation, which have been set up in accordance with its political organisation, or take the place of collective bargaining processes;

(j) allowing for the special conditions of each country, to include among the fields of competence particularly suited to tripartite co-operation policies relating to wages, industrial relations, social security, promotion of equal rights, occupational safety and health, protection of migrant workers, conditions of work, participation in the process of economic and social planning under conditions of economic and political independence, inflation, vocational training, productivity and the protection of the environment with particular reference to the work environment;

(k) to give special attention to the use of tripartite co-operation as a means of strengthening international technical co-operation and subregional integration schemes;

(l) to consider with particular interest the establishment of national tripartite machinery to assist governments to improve the implementation of ILO standards and to advise governments regarding the ratification possibilities of other ILO instruments;

(m) to apply the principles of tripartism to the methods of participation existing in the government and in the public sector of each country.

Recommends the International Labour Office and the American States Members of the International Labour Organisation to give special attention to the study of other modes and practices of co-operation, consultation and participation which, within the spirit of tripartism, have arisen in the region.

Resolution of the 10th Conference of American States Members of the ILO, Mexico, 1974

# D. Conclusions and other instruments adopted by industrial committees, experts meetings and other technical meetings convened by the ILO Governing Body

## Labour relations and collective bargaining

### 1. Collective bargaining problems and practices on plantations and the exercise of trade union rights

The Committee on Work on Plantations of the International Labour Organisation,

Having met in Geneva, in its Seventh Session, from 8 to 16 December 1976;

Adopts this sixteenth day of December 1976 the following conclusions:

#### General principles

1. Freedom of association is an essential condition for the promotion and defence of the economic and social interests of workers and employers. This implies that all workers and employers, without any distinction whatsoever, and including the plantations sector, should have the right to form and join organisations of their own choosing.

2. Governments should, by legislation or any other appropriate measures, guarantee respect for the free exercise of trade union rights on plantations. They should create conditions favourable to the formation and the development of independent workers' and employers' organisations in that sector of activity and should recognise the essential role that workers' and employers' organisations can and must play in economic and social development. The development of strong and responsible organisations is in the mutual interest of all parties.

3. Laws or other measures adopted to this end should be based on the principles contained in the relevant international labour standards and, in particular, in the Freedom of Association and Protection of the Right to Organise Convention, 1948 (No. 87), the Right to Organise and Collective Bargaining Convention, 1949 (No. 98), the Plantations Convention, 1958 (No. 110), the Rural Workers' Organisations Convention (No. 141), and Recommendation (No. 149), 1975.

4. The principles of freedom of association should be fully respected and governments should refrain from interfering in the internal affairs of workers' and employers' organisations in accordance with the relevant provisions of Convention No. 87. Workers' and employers' organisations should not interfere in each other's internal affairs. Structural changes in employers' and workers' organisations should be decided upon by the organisations themselves.

### Development of workers' and employers' organisations

5. To further the development of strong and independent workers' organisations in the plantations sector, educational and training programmes are indispensable. These programmes should not only seek to raise the general educational level of plantation workers, so that competent trade union leaders may be found among them, but should also provide special programmes of trade union education.

6. Training programmes for managerial and supervisory staff are also required to facilitate the conduct of sound labour relations, including the acceptance of trade unions representing their workers, and collective bargaining.

7. Workers' and employers' education programmes should be primarily the responsibility of their respective organisations. Nevertheless, tripartite efforts may also be developed by the government, employers' organisations and trade unions, adapted to the particular needs of the industry.

8. In order that trade unions may play an effective role, there is a need to strengthen their financial position. The check-off of union dues can be a useful system to this end provided that it is carried out with the written consent of the workers.

9. Plantation employers' and workers' organisations should, if they so desire, be entitled to affiliate with any such federation or confederation that they may choose, including central trade unions covering various sections of activity.

### Protection of trade union rights

10. Appropriate measures should be adopted to effectively protect plantation workers against any kind of anti-trade union discrimination both at the time of recruitment and during their employment.

11. In order that they may effectively perform their functions as workers' representatives, special protection and facilities should be given in this respect to plantation workers' trade union representatives in accordance with the provisions of the Workers' Representatives Convention (No. 135) and Recommendation (No. 143), 1971.

12. Governments should ensure that trade union representatives are allowed access to plantations for the legal exercise of their trade union functions on the condition that the work, during working hours, does not suffer and that the protection of property rights is fully guaranteed.

13. Where a government has acquired an interest in or ownership of undertakings in this sector, workers should enjoy full trade union rights and the public authorities should ensure the free exercise of these rights by the workers employed in such undertakings.

### Promotion of collective bargaining

14. It is desirable that conditions of work on plantations be determined by collective bargaining whether plantations are state-owned or under private ownership. Where minimum conditions are determined by law, collective bargaining should

be regarded as a means for improving the conditions of work and life of plantation workers.

15. In principle, the union representing the majority of organised workers in the undertaking should be recognised by the employer as the sole representative of the workers for bargaining purposes.

16. In order to facilitate the initiation of collective bargaining, national labour legislation should establish procedures to ensure that the parties are obliged to meet and to begin negotiations within a specified time should either party so request.

17. To facilitate meaningful collective bargaining, governments should make available to employers' and workers' organisations the necessary data concerning the economic situation of the country with a view to guiding them in their negotiations.

18. Employers should be required to furnish to the trade union representing their workers all useful data including the published financial results and prospects of the undertaking, so that collective bargaining may take place on a realistic basis. Such data should be in a form that is easily understandable to workers and trade union representatives.

19. To resolve deadlocks and settle disputes expeditiously and effectively, adequate machinery for the conciliation, mediation, arbitration or adjudication of such matters should be established by the national authorities with the agreement of workers' and employers' organisations.

20. In case of failure to settle a dispute by other means, the parties should be free to proceed to direct action, within the limits of the restraints imposed by law. Such action should, nevertheless, be taken only as a last resort. Every effort should be made to establish a climate of mutual respect and confidence that will render such action unnecessary and enable both parties to collaborate in promoting the country's development.

## Scope and contents of collective agreements

21. All matters directly affecting the conditions of work and terms of employment of workers on plantations should be negotiable. The scope of collective agreements may also include matters such as health and welfare services, workers' housing, provision of schools for their children, recreational and cultural facilities.

22. Collective agreements at the undertaking and industry-wide levels are also a suitable means of establishing clearly the relations, rights, obligations and responsibilities of the parties concerned, where these are not already defined in legislation or agreements at the national level.

23. Procedures for the processing of grievances or disputes over failure to implement the terms of an agreement should also be laid down in the agreement itself. In this connection, the provisions relating to grievance procedures contained in the Conclusions (No. 51) concerning practical measures to promote good labour-management relations on plantations, adopted by the Committee on Work on Plantations at its Fifth Session in 1966, remain valid.

24. Collective negotiations in plantations in developing countries must take into account the need to improve the position of the economy as a whole and particularly to improve the conditions of work of plantation workers. Collective

negotiations in plantations should, in so far as possible, strive for the principle of monthly wages.

### Institutional framework for collective bargaining

25. Governments should take measures to promote and facilitate the process of collective bargaining by establishing a framework of laws and institutions, adapted to the political, economic and social structure of the country concerned, relating to trade union recognition, the initiation and procedures of bargaining, dispute settlement procedures, and the status and enforceability of collective agreements. The State should not intervene directly in collective bargaining negotiations, which should be a voluntary process, but governments should provide supporting services in the form of statistical information, guidelines and assistance in resolving disputes.

26. To assist governments in developing these institutions and services, and to encourage the parties to make increased use of collective bargaining as a means of improving the conditions of work and life of plantation workers, the ILO should expand and bring up to date the international standards embodied in the Collective Agreements Recommendation, 1951 (No. 91).

Conclusions of the Committee on Work in Plantations, Seventh Session, 1976.

## 2. Industrial relations and collective bargaining practices in the chemical industries

The Chemical Industries Committee of the International Labour Organisation,

Having met in Geneva, in its Ninth Session, from 21 to 30 September 1982,

Having discussed the report (Report III) on "Industrial Relations and Collective Bargaining Practices in the Chemical Industries" which had been prepared by the International Labour Office,

Recalling the resolution (No. 32) concerning industrial relations in the chemical industries adopted by the Chemical Industries Committee at its Fifth Session,

Considering that the full respect of the right of workers and employers as set out in the Freedom of Association and Protection of the Right to Organise Convention, 1948 (No. 87) and the Right to Organise and Collective Bargaining Convention, 1949 (No. 98), can serve as a sound basis for the promotion of good industrial relations in the chemical industries,

Recalling that the International Labour Conference has adopted the Consultation (Industrial and National Levels) Recommendation, 1960 (No. 113), the Communications within the Undertaking Recommendation, 1967 (No. 129), the Examination of Grievances Recommendation, 1967 (No. 130), the Workers' Representatives Convention, 1971 (No. 135), the Workers' Representatives Recommendation, 1971 (No. 143), the Collective Bargaining Convention, 1981 (No. 154), the Collective Bargaining Recommendation, 1981 (No. 163), the Termination of Employment Convention, 1982 (No. 158) and the Termination of Employment Recommendation, 1982 (No. 166),

Noting that recent developments in the chemical industries affect industrial relations;

Adopts this thirtieth day of September 1982, the following conclusions:

## Collective bargaining

### Basic principles and the prerequisites

1. While differences existing in national laws, employment practices and cultural traditions have led to the development of various practices of industrial relations in the chemical industries in different countries, collective bargaining, as defined in Article 2 of the Collective Bargaining Convention, 1981 (No. 154), is a good means of dealing with problems confronting the chemical industries. Therefore, the principles of collective bargaining, as set out in the Collective Bargaining Convention, 1981 (No. 154), and the Collective Bargaining Recommendation, 1981 (No. 163), should be considered as a guide for the conduct of employers, employers' organisations, trade unions and/or other workers' representatives in the chemical industries in all countries.

2. An effective contribution to the development of collective bargaining in the chemical industries can be made through the establishment, on a voluntary basis, of free, independent and representative employers' organisations, trade unions and/or other workers' representatives. Governments should, therefore, endeavour to ensure the full application of the principles of freedom of association set forth in the Freedom of Association and Protection of the Right to Organise Convention, 1948 (No. 87), and the Right to Organise and Collective Bargaining Convention, 1949 (No. 98).

### Level of collective bargaining

3. The question as to what is the appropriate level for collective bargaining can best be decided by the parties.

### Authority of negotiators

4. At whatever level collective bargaining takes place, parties should provide their respective negotiators with sufficient authority to conduct negotiations and enter into agreements.

### Disclosure of information

5. The provision of requisite information by employers or employers' organisations to trade unions and/or other workers' representatives will greatly enhance the possibility of reaching agreement and mutual understanding. Employers and/or employers' organisations should provide in good faith to the trade unions and/or

other workers' representatives such information as necessary for meaningful negotiations.

*Subjects of collective bargaining*

6. Wages and other conditions of employment have traditionally been, and still remain, among the main subjects in collective bargaining in the chemical industries. Although the methods of their fixing vary considerably from country to country, employers, employers' organisations and the trade unions and/or other workers' representatives in each country should make every effort to achieve fair conditions of employment.

7. Approaches to wage indexation vary significantly from country to country and from industry to industry. The parties to collective bargaining in the chemical industries in each country should be left free to decide whether or not there should be clauses in their collective agreements providing for automatic or semi-automatic adjustment of wages to the movements in the cost of living.

8. Governments should avoid interfering in the process of collective bargaining.

*The role of governments in collective bargaining*

9. The government should play an advisory role in collective bargaining and try to bring the two parties together, as mentioned in paragraph 16 below.

*Duration of collective agreements*

10. The duration of collective agreements should be a matter for the parties to decide freely.

## Workers' participation

11. Workers' participation can normally lead to better industrial relations in the chemical industries and should therefore be promoted in the chemical industries throughout the world. However, given the variety of approaches to workers' participation, the choice of any particular method should take into account the national circumstances of each country.

12. Workers' participation requires adequate information being made available.

13. Moreover, in order to overcome the current economic recession, which is also affecting the chemical industries, it is necessary that governments, employers and trade unions and/or other workers' representatives co-operate among themselves.

14. However, workers' participation should not be a substitute for, or a device to undermine, collective bargaining.

15. If workers' participation is to contribute to improving industrial relations in the chemical industries, relevant and adequate training should be given to those involved.

## Settlement of labour disputes

16. Bodies and procedures for the settlement of labour disputes should be so conceived as to contribute to the promotion of collective bargaining. In settling labour disputes, preference should be given to procedures in which employers and employers' organisations and trade unions and/or other workers' representatives voluntarily participate rather than to compulsory procedures. Therefore, subject to national law and practice, the role of the government should be limited to the provision of procedures for dispute settlement should the parties to desire voluntarily after their own procedures have been exhausted or are otherwise not available.

Conclusions of the Chemical Industries Committee, Ninth Session, 1982.

## 3. Collective bargaining as a means of improving the working and living conditions of workers in the metal trades

The Metal Trades Committee of the International Labour Organisation,

Having met in Geneva, in its Eleventh Session, from 20 to 29 September 1983,

Having discussed the report (Report II) on "Collective Bargaining as a Means of Improving the Working and Living Conditions of Workers in the Metal Trades", which had been prepared by the International Labour Office,

Recalling the Freedom of Association and Protection of the Right to Organise Convention, 1948 (No. 87), the Right to Organise and Collective Bargaining Convention, 1949 (No. 98), the Collective Agreements Recommendation, 1951 (No. 91), the Collective Bargaining Convention, 1981 (No. 154), and the Collective Bargaining Recommendation, 1981 (No. 163),

Noting that collective bargaining, in its various forms, is a very widespread practice in the metal trades in the majority of the countries of the world,

Considering that collective bargaining is a flexible and practical machinery which the two sides of industry have at their disposal for reaching agreements with a view to fixing working and living conditions,

Noting that recent developments in the metal trades have demonstrated the effectiveness of collective bargaining as a means of resolving social problems as well as an instrument for achieving social consensus and as a mechanism for settling industrial disputes,

Adopts this twenty-ninth day of September 1983, the following conclusions:

1. While the diversity of national laws and practices in the field of industrial relations have led to the development of varying collective bargaining practices in the metal trades in different countries, collective bargaining is generally a very effective means of improving the working and living conditions of workers in the metal trades.

2. The importance which must be attached to collective bargaining as a means of fixing working conditions in no way detracts from the role that legislation plays in the matter. The law should provide minimum social guarantees to every worker irrespective of the enterprise, industry or branch of activity in which he is employed and, in particular, it should protect workers not covered by collective agreements.

3. The right to collective bargaining of all workers and employers in the metal trades should be recognised in keeping with the provisions of ILO Conventions and Recommendations on freedom of association and trade union rights. In order to ensure the exercise of the right to collective bargaining, workers should have the right to set up organisations of their own choosing independent of the employers and of the public authorities.

## Determining the content of collective agreements

4. According to the principle of voluntary negotiation laid down in Article 4 of the Right to Organise and Collective Bargaining Convention, 1949 (No. 98), the parties to collective bargaining should be free to determine, within the limits of law and public order, the content of their agreements and, consequently, to agree on the clauses relating to all the working and living conditions. They could, in particular, improve upon the minimum standards guaranteed by the law as well as agree on other social benefits or guarantees not provided for under the legislation.

5. Governments should avoid interfering in the process of collective bargaining. Their role should be to establish minimum conditions of work and to provide an appropriate framework so that collective bargaining between the two sides might proceed without difficulty.

## The level of collective bargaining

6. It should be for the two sides to choose the most appropriate level for collective bargaining on working conditions in the metal trades. According to the principle laid down in Paragraph 4(2) of the Collective Bargaining Recommendation, 1981 (No. 163), in countries where collective negotiations take place at more than one level, the parties involved should seek to ensure co-ordination between the various levels.

## Collective bargaining in the face of economic recession and structural and technical changes in the metal trades

7. Industrial relations in the metal trades are pursued, at present, under the combined influence of several factors including technological change, increased international competition and economic recession affecting a very large number of countries. The survival of enterprises is frequently linked with the response to be given to the economic and technological challenge. These factors should be taken into consideration when the social partners try to solve problems such as maintaining the competitive position of the enterprise and the introduction of new technologies. Account should also be taken of the interest in protecting employment and improving working conditions and wage standards.

8. Although the economic crisis and the structural and technological changes affecting the metal trades have raised severe problems during the last few years, the fact remains that collective bargaining continues to be the most appropriate machinery for the discussion of the problems related to work and employment as well

as for the solution of industrial disputes and, where necessary, for the promotion of social consensus.

9. Both sides should negotiate bearing in mind the overall economic and social situation especially when collective bargaining may lead to results that could affect the national economy. Nevertheless both sides should be free to arrive at their own decisions in accordance with the principles of bilateral and voluntary collective bargaining.

## Wage bargaining

10. The parties to collective bargaining should be in a position to negotiate on all wage questions.

11. Public authorities should avoid interfering in wage negotiations. Any state intervention in collective bargaining should be the subject of prior negotiations with the two sides of industry or failing that, if possible, of consultations in keeping with the principles set forth in the Consultation (Industrial and National Levels) Recommendation, 1960 (No. 113). In accordance with the criteria established by the ILO supervisory organs, any binding state intervention on the grounds of a policy stabilisation should be regarded as an exceptional measure, be limited to the indispensable, be of reasonable duration and be accompanied by appropriate safeguards to protect the standing of living of the workers.

## Negotiations concerning job security

12. The parties should be able to negotiate the inclusion, in their collective agreements, of clauses regulating individual dismissals, particularly in countries which have no legislation on the subject or where such legislation only affords limited basic protection to the worker. To this end, they might bear in mind, in particular, the standards set out in the Termination of Employment Convention, 1982 (No. 158), and the Termination of Employment Recommendation, 1982 (No. 166).

13. In the light of the technological and economic trends, a large number of negotiations which have taken place in metal trades over the past few years have placed emphasis on employment problems. This being so and in the absence of appropriate general regulations and without prejudice to the social programmes of industrial restructuring or to the bipartite or tripartite negotiations and consultations at the level of the branch of activity—or at the national level—aimed at solving the unemployment problem, the parties should be able to negotiate, at the enterprise or plant level, procedures to be applied in handling questions relating to collective dismissals for economic, technological, structural or similar reasons. To this end, they should draw inspiration from the standards contained in the Termination of Employment Convention, 1982 (No. 158), and the Termination of Employment Recommendation, 1982 (No. 166).

## Negotiations on hours of work

14. The parties to collective bargaining should be able to negotiate on the various questions relating to hours of work or the arrangement of working time, such

as daily, weekly, monthly or annual hours of work, overtime, holidays with pay, time off with or without pay, early retirement, part-time work, rest periods, flexible working hours, night work and shift work.

15. Although there is disagreement about the effectiveness of reduction in working time as a weapon in the fight against unemployment, one might nevertheless regard such a reduction as an objective to be achieved within the framework of policies for the improvement of working conditions. The scope for further reduction of working time in the metal trades differs widely from country to country owing to the great differences between their economic and social situations. In this regard, collective bargaining, because of its flexibility, is an excellent means allowing the parties to handle the problems realistically, thus taking into account both the social interest in shortening the working hours as well as the economic implications for the enterprise.

## Negotiations on work reorganisation and the introduction of new technologies

16. At the present time it seems clear that the survival of enterprises in the metal trades will depend, in a large measure, on the manner in which they are able to adapt themselves to technological change. Nevertheless, the introduction of new technologies may have an impact on employment, job content, work organisation and plant systems design, working conditions, health, occupational classification and wages of workers. In accordance with national law and practice, both sides of industry could negotiate framework agreements with a view to handling social problems arising from the introduction of new technologies. To this end they should draw inspiration from the standards contained in the Termination of Employment Convention, 1982 (No. 158), and the Termination of Employment Recommendation, 1982 (No. 166).

## Negotiations on occupational safety and health

17. Safety and health are essential to working conditions as well as a subject of concern both to workers and employers as well as governments. Even in times of economic recession and technological change safety and health standards must not be set aside. Consequently, the protection of workers against occupational hazards should be the subject of technical standards which all employers and workers should respect. The control of the application of these standards should be ensured by the government. In this context, the objective of collective bargaining might be to fill gaps as far as necessary in the general regulations and to establish, if necessary, measures to facilitate the practical application of safety and health standards at the level of the enterprise, plant or workshop. In accordance with national law and practice, such measures might include provisions relating to the functioning of safety and health committees, the facilities to be given to their members, training sessions in the utilisation of protective equipment or any other measures which the parties may consider necessary. The ILO plays an important role in this field. It should actively continue to support the social partners and governments accordingly.

## Negotiations on social services within undertakings

18. Without prejudice to the role of the state in organisation of social welfare services for the community as a whole, social services within undertakings can make an important contribution to the improvement of living conditions of workers, particularly in developing countries. In accordance with national law and practice, collective agreements, particularly at the level of the enterprise or the plant, could include clauses relating to social services within the undertakings such as enterprise canteens, supplementary social security schemes, leisure or other social services which, under usual practice, are provided by the employer. The Utilisation of Spare Time Recommendation, 1924 (No. 21), the Welfare Facilities Recommendation, 1956 (No. 102), and the Workers' Housing Recommendation, 1961 (No. 115), are to be observed in this regard.

## Future international action

19. The Committee notes that bargaining on possible adverse effects of new technologies on workers is a rather new issue. It considers that this question should be thoroughly examined by the Office in the coming years.

Conclusions of the Metal Trade Committee, Eleventh Session, 1983.

# Labour relations in the public service

## 1. Disciplinary codes and procedures in the public service and conditions of work and employment of public service personnel of local, regional or provincial authorities

The Joint Committee on the Public Service,

Having been convened by the Governing Body of the ILO, and

Having met in its Second Session in Geneva from 6 to 13 April 1976, and

Having noted with approval the conclusions of the Technical Conference on the Public Service held in 1975, and

Having noted with appreciation the action of the Governing Body to place the conclusions of the 1975 Technical Conference on the Public Service before the 1977 Session of the International Labour Conference with a view to the adoption of a suitable international instrument, and

Referring to the Termination of Employment Recommendation, 1963, and the ILO-UNESCO Recommendation concerning the status of teachers, 1966, and

Recognising the great diversity among national laws and constitutions governing conditions of work and employment at the local, regional and provincial levels, and

Stressing that public employees are entitled to fair and equitable conditions of employment, that the public service requires the highest conduct and performance by public employees and that fair and equitable disciplinary practices contribute to the effective conduct of the public's business;

Adopts, this thirteenth day of April 1976, the following conclusions:

### I. Disciplinary codes and procedures in the public service

#### General principles

1. The preparation, establishment and amendment of disciplinary codes and procedures should be effected with the participation of appropriate organisations representing public servants, in accordance with the principles which were accepted by the Technical Conference on the Public Service in 1975.

2. Public authorities should define in clear and concise language, free from ambiguity and not susceptible to misinterpretation, a code of conduct for all their employees. An obligation to obey the orders of a superior should be invoked only in connection with instructions regarding the official work of the public authority concerned.

3. Disciplinary procedures may only be undertaken against public servants where there has been a clear breach of the code of conduct referred to in the previous paragraph. In no circumstances may a breach be established on the basis of race, colour, sex or religion, nor on the basis of the exercise of civil and political rights,

subject, however, to the obligations arising from their status and the nature of their functions.

4. No disciplinary procedures may be undertaken nor sanctions imposed on account of normal trade union activities protected by ILO principles and relevant international instruments and construed in the light of the conclusions of the Technical Conference on the Public Service held in April 1975.

5. There must be no unwarranted intrusion into the private lives of public servants. A public servant convicted of an act unrelated to his official duties should not also be liable to disciplinary sanctions unless such conviction has itself raised doubts about his fitness as a public servant.

6. While any criminal charge is under investigation, in principle no disciplinary sanction should be brought against the public servant concerned, unless the alleged misconduct independently contravenes the code of conduct.

*Procedures*

7. Disciplinary procedures must fulfil at least the following criteria:
(a) disciplinary procedures against a public servant must be precisely defined and based on a breach of the code of conduct. The nature of the charges should be made clear to him and, at his request, to the trade union representative who may represent him;
(b) trade union organisations must be entitled, in principle, to assist in the defence of the employee, at his request, in answering the charges made at all stages of the procedure; every public servant must have the right to be defended by his trade union or by a person of his choice at each stage of the disciplinary procedure and, in particular:
  (i) the right to be fully informed of the allegations and the grounds for them;
  (ii) the right to appeal to a higher authority, so that his case is given fair, speedy and impartial treatment;
(c) when making an appeal, the public servant must—
  (i) be informed in writing of the nature of the charges;
  (ii) be given an opportunity of stating his case orally before an officer of higher authority than the officer who authorised the disciplinary sanction;
  (iii) be presented with the evidence relied upon to sustain the charges which resulted in the disciplinary sanction;
  (iv) be informed of his right to be defended, if he so wishes, by a representative or by his trade union.
(d) there must be no unreasonable delay in bringing the appeal to a prompt hearing and the public servant should in no way be hindered from conducting his case in the most effective manner;
(e) once a decision to dismiss has been taken, the public servant should be given a final opportunity to make such representations as he thinks fit; if dismissal is subsequently upheld by a higher authority which has the power to dismiss, the public servant must be given notice and told of his right to appeal to an independent body within a prescribed period of time;

*(f)* the question of whether the right of appeal shall suspend imposition of the sanction shall be determined with the participation of appropriate organisations representing public servants, in accordance with the principles which were accepted by the Technical Conference on the Public Service in 1975.

### Sanctions

8. Disciplinary sanctions must be fixed by law or regulations. No sanction may be imposed if not laid down in these texts. The variety of possible disciplinary measures must be as wide as possible in order to permit in each case the sanction to be fitted in the most just manner to the offence.

9. The periods of limitation as well as the periods within which disciplinary sanctions may be withdrawn from the personnel files shall be fixed by regulations.

### Preventive suspension

10. Suspension of public servants from duty while disciplinary proceedings, or investigative and judicial proceedings concerning criminal charges, are under consideration, should be determined only in cases where it is not feasible to reassign the public servant to other duties temporarily or when it is necessary to protect the public servant, other public servants, public property or the public interest.

11. The public servant must have the right of appeal to a higher authority within the shortest time possible.

12. The question of whether public servants should be paid during the period of suspension should be determined in accordance with the procedure set out in paragraph 1 under the section entitled "General Principles".

13. In the event a public servant is acquitted of all charges that have been brought against him, his full rights should be restored.

## II. Conditions of work and employment of public service personnel of local, regional or provincial authorities

### General considerations

14. The present situation with regard to the conditions of work and employment of public service personnel of local, regional or provincial authorities shows such diversity as to warrant the adoption at the international level of a code of good practice which should serve as a guide for governments, employers and workers. This code of good practice should be incorporated as soon as possible into a suitable international labour instrument.

15. The comparisons between local authority employees and central government employees, whilst showing many areas of similarity, display many differences in treatment which could be regarded as being inconsistent with the services rendered to the community by each group. Where these differences result in an unfair treatment of

public employees, remedial action should be taken by the appropriate competent authority.

*General principles*

16. In regard to matters not subject to national laws and regulations, conditions of employment for local, regional and provincial personnel are best determined by the competent authorities at that level. Whatever principles and procedures for determining conditions of employment are adopted in any forthcoming international instrument on the public service should be considered appropriate at these levels of government in respect of these matters.

17. Regardless of the methods of determination of the conditions of employment existing in different member States, the conditions of employment should be consistent with career systems. It should be the role of the national government to provide a basis for the development and improvement of such systems permitting lawful involvement of public employees and their organisations in appropriate matters of concern.

18. The conditions of work and employment of such employees should be clearly defined as should the methods of determining these conditions, which should be directed towards conformity of conditions of service for those employees providing comparable standards of service to the public.

*Career system*

19. The career system must be clearly defined so that some assessment of the qualities and conditions required for advancement can be made and be seen to present avenues giving enough scope for regular progress. In the career structure, the training and potential of the employee should be taken into consideration, in order to afford the freedom and the opportunity to transfer to some other form of activity, and for progression over a wide and varied field.

*Recruitment*

20. The competent legislative authorities should establish common standards of recruitment for local public employees and conditions of entry should be free from all forms of discrimination.

21. Priority for recruitment of senior and specialist staff should be given to applicants from within the service.

22. A probationary period should be established for the purpose of evaluating the capacity of the employees on the basis of predefined rules. Where the employee is unsuitable for the original assignment, he should be given the opportunity of applying for another post.

23. Recruitment of temporary or unestablished staff should be restricted to those areas where the employment is for a limited period. Non-established staff who have been in employment for a long period should be given the opportunity to

become established and to pursue a normal career. Service as non-established staff should be taken into account in calculating length of service.

### Training

24. The increasing complexity of the demands of a modern public service and the advances in the use of technology should be adequately reflected in training policy. Training programmes should be designed to fulfil as many specialist requirements as possible to avoid the need to bring in outside expertise.

25. Local public employees should be given an initial orientation programme, whenever appropriate, and the opportunity for further training to qualify them for advancement and promotion.

26. Employees should be given the opportunity to obtain further training and the advantages to the local authority of wider forms of educational training should not be ignored. Paid educational leave should be applied under the conditions of the Paid Educational Leave Convention (No. 140) and Recommendation (No. 148), 1974.

27. The internal, general and vocational training programme (including workers' education) should be designed to guide the employee to combine serving the best interests of the public with his ambitions to advance his career.

### Advancement and promotion

28. The opportunity for advancement and promotion is one of the highest priorities, and a clearly defined, well understood system should be amongst the conditions of service.

29. The system should include some form of appeals machinery.

30. Alongside with professional qualifications, merit and seniority should be an important element in deciding advancement.

### Discipline

31. The above conclusions on disciplinary codes and procedures should apply to public employees of local, provincial or regional authorities.

### Security of employment

32. Security of employment should be a fundamental principle in the employment of local, regional and provincial public employees. In accordance with the Termination of Employment Recommendation, 1963, no dismissal of established employees should occur unless there is a valid reason.

### Remuneration

33. The remuneration of public employees of local, regional or provincial authorities should be sufficient to attract and retain suitably qualified personnel.

34. Its level should be determined and adjusted in relation to the remuneration offered in the national public service and in other sectors at the local, regional and provincial levels and to the general economic and financial situation. It should also be adapted, where appropriate, in the light of merit and performance.

*Hours of work and overtime*

35. The normal hours of work for public employees of local, regional or provincial authorities should be established in accordance with general practice. It should be progressively reduced to 40 hours a week, where this period is exceeded, and should be spread over not more than five working days per week. Improvements in the arrangement of hours of work, including flexible time, should be periodically reviewed.

36. Strict limits should be introduced in respect of the total number of hours of overtime to be authorised over a given period. Overtime should normally be compensated by extra remuneration, which should be fixed at a sufficiently high level to discourage extended use of overtime, or by compensatory time off. The level of compensation and limitation of overtime should be periodically reviewed.

*Holidays*

37. Public employees of local, regional or provincial authorities should be entitled to annual holidays, the length of which and payment for should reflect general practices. The aim should be to progressively increase the minimum period of leave to four weeks per year. Remuneration during leave should not be less than the normal earnings basis.

38. The scheduling of annual leave should recognise both the requirements of the service and the needs of the employee. Employees should be encouraged to take their annual leave, which should only be exceptionally and partially deferred to the following year.

*ILO action*

39. Since workers employed in the water, gas and electricity services within the public sector, who in many countries come under the authority of a local administration, were not covered by the studies prepared for the present session, the conditions of work and employment of these workers should be considered by a Joint Committee of Experts at the earliest opportunity.

Conclusions of the Joint Committee on the Public Service, Second Session, 1976

## 2. Labour disputes and procedures for their settlement in the public service

The Meeting on the Settlement of Labour Disputes in the Public Service,
Having been convened by the Governing Body of the ILO,

Having met in Geneva from 6 to 10 October 1986,

Noting that public service labour disputes are an important issue in many countries,

Noting the significant increase in the number and intensity of public service labour disputes in many countries in recent years, resulting from a variety of causes and their impact on public service labour relations,

adopts this tenth day of October 1986 the following conclusions:

1. Appropriate means for avoiding labour disputes as far as possible and for settling those that arise are essential to the existence of sound and constructive labour relations in the public service which in turn is necessary to the maintenance of efficient service to the public.

2. Sound and constructive labour relations in the public service, including the avoidance and settlement of labour disputes, should be achieved, in particular, within the framework of respect for the fundamental principles of freedom of association included in the Freedom of Association and Protection of the Right to Organise Convention, 1948 (No. 87), the Right to Organise and Collective Bargaining Convention, 1949 (No. 98), and the Labour Relations (Public Service) Convention, 1978 (No. 151), to the extent that they apply to the public service, and on the basis of mutual understanding of the parties to public service labour relations.

3. While these principles should be respected in all countries in the public service, there can be no uniform model of public service labour relations applicable to all countries and each has to evolve the system best suited to its national legal, institutional, social and economic conditions.

4. The avoidance and timely settlement of labour disputes requires that there be appropriate means of involving public servants' organisations in the determination of terms and conditions of employment of their members, whether through negotiation or through such other methods as will allow representatives of public servants to participate in the determination of these matters, in accordance with Article 7 of Convention No. 151.

5. The settlement of labour disputes arising in connection with the determination of terms and conditions of employment in the public service should be sought, as may be appropriate to national conditions, through negotiation between the parties or through independent and impartial machinery, such as mediation, conciliation and arbitration, established in such a manner as to ensure the confidence of the parties involved, as provided by Article 8 of Convention No. 151. In this connection, consideration should be given also to the standards contained in the Voluntary Conciliation and Arbitration Recommendation, 1951 (No. 92).

6. The settlement of labour disputes is facilitated when the choice of the means available and the position of the parties are sufficiently flexible and well balanced, so that the procedure followed can be best adapted to the particular circumstances of each dispute.

7. The parties to public service labour relations should review, at appropriate intervals, the functioning of the machinery for the settlement of labour disputes, having regard to the evolution of labour relations generally and labour disputes in particular in the public service, with a view to determining whether improvements are needed.

Conclusions of the Meeting in the Public Service, the settlement of Labour Disputes, Geneva, 1986

## 3. Joint consultation, negotiating and collective bargaining rights with regard to determining pay and conditions of employment in the public service

The Joint Committee on the Public Service of the International Labour Organisation,

Having met in Geneva, in its Fourth Session, from 23 November to 1 December 1988,

Noting that collective bargaining, negotiating and joint consultation rights with regard to determining pay and conditions of employment in the public service are an essential aspect of trade union rights in the public service, since one of the main purposes of the right to organise is to guarantee workers the right to participate effectively in determining their terms and conditions of employment,

Noting that this subject has acquired considerable significance in many countries because of the importance of the public service and because of the difficulties arising in public service labour relations in recent years,

Noting that considerable progress has been made in many countries over the past decades in extending to public employees the right to participate in determining their conditions of employment, while little progress has been made in others and in some countries the rights previously recognised have to some extent been restricted or suspended not only in the context of government austerity measures taken in situations of economic constraint,

Noting the considerable diversity in public service labour relations systems in member countries of the ILO, resulting from differing constitutional, political, cultural and labour relations traditions,

Noting that public service labour relations systems in different countries are continually evolving and will continue to do so,

Recalling the Meeting on the Settlement of Labour Disputes in the Public Service held in Geneva in October 1986,

Adopts this first day of December 1988 the following conclusions:

1. The right of workers to establish and join organisations of their own choosing must be enjoyed by public employees, in accordance with the Freedom of Association and Protection of the Right to Organise Convention, 1948 (No. 87).

2. Workers in the public service must enjoy effective protection against acts of anti-union discrimination in respect of their employment, in accordance with the provisions of the Right to Organise and Collective Bargaining Convention, 1949 (No. 98), and of the Labour Relations (Public Service) Convention, 1978 (No. 151).

3. Public employees must enjoy the right to participate effectively through collective bargaining or other appropriate means in the determination of their conditions of employment, in accordance with the provisions of the Right to Organise and Collective Bargaining Convention, 1949 (No. 98), the Labour Relations (Public Service) Convention, 1978 (No. 151), and the Collective Bargaining Convention, 1981 (No. 154).

4. Procedures for the effective participation of representatives of public employees must extend to the determination of as many questions affecting their conditions of employment as possible.

5. On issues with regard to which the prerogatives of the legislature must be respected in the decision-making process concerning the conditions of employment of public employees, ways should be sought to reconcile the requirements of the legislative prerogatives with those of effective public employee participation.

6. Where collective negotiation procedures are followed, measures should be taken by the parties to ensure that their negotiators have the opportunity to obtain appropriate training for the purpose of negotiation, in accordance with the Collective Bargaining Recommendation, 1981 (No. 163).

7. Where collective negotiation procedures are followed, in order for the process to be successful it is necessary that the parties provide their representatives with the appropriate mandate, in accordance with Recommendation No. 163.

8. Measures adapted to national conditions should be taken if necessary so that the parties have access to the information required for meaningful participation, in accordance with Recommendation No. 163.

9. Appropriate recognition of the right of public employees to organise and for their representatives to participate effectively in the determination of their conditions of employment, and respect for these rights in practice, are conducive to the avoidance of labour disputes. Where labour disputes, including strikes, arise in connection with the determination of conditions of employment, their settlement should be sought, as may be appropriate to national conditions, through negotiation between the parties or through independent and impartial machinery, such as mediation, conciliation and arbitration, established in such a manner as to ensure the confidence of the parties involved, in accordance with Convention No. 151.

10. Measures should be taken by the ILO, whether in its relationship with the international financial institutions or in its relationship with the countries concerned or both, to help ensure that the conditions associated with granting assistance to these countries by the international financial institutions do not unduly diminish conditions of employment in the public service nor undermine the process of effective public employee participation in determining those conditions. More generally, where governments apply austerity policies in the public service, they should seek to ensure that the process of public employee participation in determining their conditions of employment is not undermined.

11. The parties to public service labour relations should review, at appropriate intervals, the functioning of the procedures for the participation of public employee representatives in the determination of public employees' conditions of employment and of the machinery for the settlement of labour disputes, as well as the scope of issues subject to these procedures, having regard to the evolution of labour relations generally in the public service, with a view to determining whether changes are needed.

Conclusions of the Joint Committee on the Public Service, 4th Session, 1988

## Labour relations in health and medical services

### 1. Employment, labour-management relations, remuneration, ethical problems, working time and occupational health and safety in health and medical services

The Joint Meeting on Employment and Conditions of Work in Health and Medical Services,

Having been convened by the Governing Body of the ILO,

Having met in Geneva from 8 to 15 October 1985;

Adopts this fifteenth day of October 1985, the following conclusions:

[...]

#### Labour-management relations

15. The right of workers to organise in trade unions of their own choosing, as enshrined in the Freedom of Association and Protection of the Right to Organise Convention, 1948 (No. 87), should be universally accepted for all workers in the health and medical services sector.

16. In circumstances where freedom of association is denied or restricted for workers in health and medical services, measures should be taken to ensure that all workers in these services may freely exercise the right to organise.

17. Representatives of workers in health and medical services should enjoy effective protection against acts of anti-union discrimination in respect of their employment. They should also be afforded such facilities as may be appropriate to enable them to carry out their functions promptly and efficiently, in accordance with the provisions of the Workers' Representatives Convention, 1971 (No. 135).

18. The practice of collective bargaining has been expanding in health and medical services in a number of countries, and the right of workers to bargain collectively is now recognised in most countries. This right is, however, restricted in some cases, particularly in the public sector; these restrictions hinder full participation by workers in health and medical services and their representatives in the determination of their employment and working conditions through collective bargaining.

19. Measures should be taken, where necessary, to encourage and promote the full development of machinery for voluntary negotiations between employers and workers and their representatives, with a view to the regulation of terms and conditions of employment by means of collective bargaining, as laid down in the Right to Organise and Collective Bargaining Convention, 1949 (No. 98), and reaffirmed in the Labour Relations (Public Service) Convention, 1978 (No. 151), and the Collective Bargaining Convention, 1981 (No. 154).

20. The development of procedures for the speedy settlement of labour disputes arising in connection with the determination of terms and conditions of employment is a subject of major concern for both employers and workers in health

and medical services, since both parties recognise the need to ensure the uninterrupted provision of essential health care to the public.

21. In accordance with the opinion expressed by the Committee on Freedom of Association, the right to strike by workers and their organisations is a legitimate means of defending their economic and social interests. However, the Committee has said that this right may be restricted, in particular in essential services in the strict sense of the term, i.e. services the interruption of which would endanger the life, personal safety or health of the whole or part of the population. In several countries, the right to strike is recognised in some health and medical services. In other countries, these services, being considered essential, are subject to restrictions on the right to strike. In case of work stoppages, a minimum service concerning specified categories of workers may be deemed justified since a total stoppage of work in these services may be such as to endanger the life, safety or health of persons in need of health care. Workers' representatives should be able to participate effectively in defining such minimum service.

22. Owing to the nature of the work of medical and health service workers and its importance for the life, personal safety or health of persons in their care, reasonable pay and conditions of work should always apply in order to reduce the incidence of strikes. A major contribution to good industrial relations can be made by the introduction of speedy, impartial machinery for the resolution of disputes, particularly in those countries where the right to strike is restricted.

23. Procedures should be developed to enable workers to be informed and consulted on all matters affecting their working environment, it being recognised that some such matters in certain countries might go beyond subjects which are normally issues dealt with by collective bargaining.

## *Remuneration*

24. The remuneration of workers in health and medical services should be determined through voluntary collective bargaining between employers and the workers' representatives. In cases where arrangements do not yet exist for free collective bargaining, they should be promoted in order that all workers in health and medical services, through their representatives, may benefit from this right.

25. Where collective bargaining leading to the determination of the remuneration of health and medical workers takes place at different levels, the parties concerned should ensure that there is co-ordination between the levels and that health and medical workers and management are represented at these different levels.

26. The remuneration of all workers employed in health and medical services should be determined on the basis of objective criteria such as the level of qualification, degree of responsibility, job requirements, job performance, nature of work, experience and length of service, as well as the specific constraints and hazards inherent in the various health professions.

27. A large number of workers in health and medical services, in particular women, earn wages which are in lower-earnings categories. They are particularly vulnerable in defending their economic interests, due to the nature of their work and their sense of responsibility and commitments to the patients in their care. All

employees in health and medical services should receive adequate levels of remuneration, so as to ensure that they and their families have an acceptable standard of living.

28. Great imbalances often prevail between the higher and lower wages paid in the sector. In order to correct unjustified imbalances, it is essential that the remuneration of workers in health and medical services reflect the real value of their work. Where sophisticated methods of determining the comparative value of work already exist and enjoy the confidence of the parties, they should be used to establish equitable pay conditions for all jobs.

29. The principle of equal pay for work of equal value should be assured to women in health and medical services in accordance with the Equal Remuneration Convention (No. 100) and Recommendation (No. 90) of 1951. This principle should be applied by ensuring a classification of jobs and promotion prospects without regard to sex.

30. Pay and grading structures should be so established as to reflect the staffing needs of health and medical services. They should normally be such as to attract adequately qualified staff in the numbers required and to encourage this staff to remain in the services by offering them the incentives for promotion.

31. Remuneration should, furthermore, be sufficiently clear to enable comparisons to be made between the various occupational groups in the sector. This also applies to indirect components of remuneration (bonuses, payments and allowances related to specific duties or conditions of work or to the cost of living), which should be considered as part of total remuneration.

32. Where comparability with the levels of remuneration applying in other sectors is a factor in determining the remuneration of health and medical staff, the methodology used for making comparisons should be clearly understood and established in such a way as to have the confidence of the parties involved. Relevant and comparable data on pay and other conditions should be equally available to all parties in the negotiations.

33. Remuneration should be periodically reviewed, taking into account fluctuations in the cost of living, changes in work organisation, increases in productivity and work performance, the acquisition of additional skills and general increases in standards of living or earnings.

34. Adequate compensation should be given to health and medical staff who work in arduous or unpleasant conditions, or in isolated or rural areas; such compensation should not, however, lead to serious distortions in prevailing earnings patterns.

[...]

Conclusions of the Joint Meeting on Employment and Conditions of Work in Health and Medical Services, 1985

STANDARDS AND GUIDING PRINCIPLES

## Employment security

### 1. Social problems of contract, subcontract and casual labour in the petroleum industry

The Petroleum Committee of the International Labour Organisation,

Having been convened by the Governing Body of the International Labour Office, and

Having met in its Eighth Session at Geneva from 2 to 13 April 1973,

Having considered the social problems of contract, sub-contract and casual labour in the petroleum industry,

Recalling that the Petroleum Committee in its Fifth Session at Caracas in April–May 1955 and at Geneva in April 1956 adopted unanimously a Resolution (No. 44) concerning Conditions of Employment of Contract Labour in the Petroleum Industry,

Noting that the provisions of that resolution have not been implemented everywhere in the petroleum industry and that the conditions to which it referred, which are prejudicial to the interests of workers in the industry, still exist in certain areas,

Considering that there is a tendency for the contracting out of work to increase in both the public and the private sectors of the petroleum industry because of technical changes requiring highly specialised personnel and equipment; that maintenance of equipment and other operations related to production processes as well as auxiliary services and clerical work, which were formerly performed by regular, permanently employed workers of oil undertakings, are frequently contracted out; that new forms of contract labour have developed; and that the employment of temporary personnel through the medium of temporary help agencies or other types of labour supply contractors is also on the increase in a number of countries,

Considering that the contracting out of work in the oil industry is often indispensable because of technical imperatives and that this practice may have useful employment creation effects and facilitate the transfer of technological know-how for the economic and social benefit of other countries,

Considering also that the increased use of contract labour may result in a lessening of the number of regular workers employed in the undertakings,

Considering further that the working conditions of the contract labour engaged in the oil industry should be regulated by law and/or collective agreements freely negotiated between the organisations of workers and employers,

Believing that governments, employers' and workers' organisations alike in the petroleum industry have a common interest, for economic, social and humanitarian reasons, in helping to ensure that contract workers are employed in satisfactory conditions and that contract labour practices do not undermine industrial relations,

Noting also that similar problems may arise in other industries with regard to the use of contract and casual labour,

Adopts this thirteenth day of April 1973 the following conclusions:

1. Taking into account national conditions, efforts should be made by the public authorities and the oil industry in order to provide better protection for those contract, subcontract and casual workers who are not adequately protected by legislation or collective agreements, giving special regard to labour contracting, in which context licensing of contractors or other limitations or even abolition might be considered, if appropriate.

2. Work involved in the technical processes of the oil industry for the performance of which equipment and permanent employees are available or can easily be made available in the undertaking concerned should not be contracted out except in unusual circumstances. Such unusual circumstances might include, for example, installation or revision work.

3. The employment of temporary or casual workers through labour supply contractors, including temporary help agencies, should be limited to temporary or unforeseeable needs for personnel; oil undertakings should, in any case, carry a sufficient complement of permanent workers to meet normal absences.

4. In cases in which the interests of the regular employees are or may be affected by contracting out, they or their representatives should be informed by the oil undertaking beforehand. Where there exist procedures of consultation or of collective bargaining applicable to the undertaking, full use should be made of such procedures.

5. Contracts entered into by the oil undertaking and the contractor should include a clause requiring the contractor to provide fair wages and working conditions for the contract labour.

6. Governments should ensure that statutory minimum standards regarding conditions of employment, including health and safety, are applicable to contract and casual labour and are effectively applied to such workers, sanctions being provided for violations of legal provisions.

7. Where contract work is carried out at remote or isolated sites, particular attention should be paid by the public authorities to the need for ensuring respect of statutory standards regarding conditions of work and safety and health; the contractor should provide or arrange, in co-operation with the oil undertaking, if necessary, for adequate medical and supply facilities and accommodation for contract labour when operating on such remote or isolated sites.

8. Where necessary, efforts should be made to guarantee to workers in contract and casual employment the full enjoyment of trade union rights.

9. Appropriate protection against unjustified dismissal should be applicable to contract and casual workers.

10. A limit may be fixed, by collective agreement, on the duration of employment of casual or temporary workers employed by oil undertakings; these workers may be integrated into the regular workforce after a certain period of time worked in the same undertaking.

11. Workers employed by contractors on the construction of new installations for the oil industry should, where appropriate and after suitable training, be offered permanent employment in those new installations when they become operational.

12. The oil undertakings should provide adequate vocational training, further training and retraining for their employees so that specialised personnel requirements

may be filled as far as possible by promotions or transfers of regular workers rather than by recourse to temporary personnel or to contractors.

Conclusions of the Petroleum Committee, Eighth Session, 1973

## 2. Employment security in civil aviation

The Tripartite Technical Meeting for Civil Aviation,

Having been convened by the Governing Body of the International Labour Office, and

Having met in Geneva from 7 to 15 December 1977,

Having examined different factors which affect employment security in civil aviation and the various measures which have been taken on different occasions by governments, employers and workers and their organisations in order to protect workers' employment security when threatened or to mitigate the adverse effects of loss of employment on the workers concerned,

Noting the principles and standards set forth in the Termination of Employment Recommendation, 1963 (No. 119), the Right to Organise and Collective Bargaining Convention, 1949 (No. 98), and the Discrimination (Employment and Occupation) Convention (No. 111) and Recommendation (No. 111) of 1958;

Adopts this fifteenth day of December 1977 the following conclusions:

### General considerations

1. Employment security in civil aviation is subject to a number of different factors, including economic factors, such as cyclical and seasonal variations in demand for air transport services, cost inflation, excess capacity, increasing competition and economic problems connected with regulation of route licensing and air fares; technological factors, including changes in equipment and aircraft and increasing computerisation and automation of operations; reorganisation or restructuring of air transport services, including mergers, co-operative arrangements, rationalisation measures and closures; and special licensing and other requirements related to health, skills and other conditions of employment of different categories engaged in the industry.

2. The civil aviation industry has a relatively good record in providing employment security for its personnel. Provision of security of employment for persons employed in the industry should remain an important objective of governments, employers, workers and their organisations.

3. Ensuring employment security in the civil aviation industry depends in large measure on ensuring the economic health and viability of the industry, which depends in part on the health of the economy in general and in part upon the viability of individual undertakings and services within the civil aviation industry.

4. Having regard to the relationship between the economics of the industry and employment security, regulatory authorities should consult air carriers and the workers' organisations concerned before deciding to grant or withdraw operating licences.

5. Constructive labour-management relations and regular consultation, in accordance with collective agreements, national law or current practice, are important to the economic health of the industry and thus also to employment security.

## Protection against dismissal

6. The employment of civil aviation workers should not be terminated unless there is a valid reason for such termination connected with the capacity or conduct of the worker or based on the operational requirements of the undertaking, establishment or service.

7. The protection laid down in the Termination of Employment Recommendation, 1963 (No. 119), should be applied to all workers in civil aviation. In general, this means that a worker who feels that his employment has been unjustifiably terminated should be entitled to appeal against that termination under a grievance procedure within the undertaking, established in accordance with collective agreements, national laws or current practice, and to impartial machinery outside the undertaking empowered to decide on the justification of the termination and to award appropriate remedies where it finds that the termination of employment was unjustified.

## Protection against or in case of loss of licence

8. Personnel subject to licensing requirements should be covered by adequate measures, which may be at the employer's expense, designed to prevent loss of licence. This protection should include the availability of appropriate medical services and training facilities to assist the persons concerned in maintaining the required health and skill standards. In the event of loss on medical grounds of a licence which includes medical standards, such measures should also include provision for income protection, such as adequate loss-of-licence insurance and, where applicable, disability insurance and retirement or early retirement pensions, in accordance with collective agreements, national laws or current practice. Opportunities for retraining and redeployment should also be available to workers who lose their licences.

## Protection against discrimination

9. Women and men should have equality of treatment in accordance with the principles set out in the Discrimination (Employment and Occupation) Convention, 1958 (No. 111).

## Protection to be afforded in case employment security is threatened for reasons of an economic, technological or organisational character

10. Workers in civil aviation and their representatives should be informed sufficiently in advance of and consulted on any appropriate proposed change in the structure, general objectives, working methods, equipment or operational plans of an undertaking which is liable to prejudice employment security.

11. Where personnel reductions are foreseen, the employer should inform the workers' representatives and the appropriate public authorities as early as possible and, in accordance with collective agreements, national laws or current practice, consult such representatives to devise measures which might be taken to avoid or limit collective dismissals or layoffs as well as measures to mitigate the adverse consequences of any personnel reductions on the workers affected.

12. The measures which should be considered with a view to avoiding or limiting collective dismissals or layoffs should include attrition, incentives to voluntary departure or early retirement, internal transfer and training, reduction of overtime and other methods as considered appropriate.

13. Having regard to the difficulty for older workers of finding alternative employment if they lose their jobs, such workers should as far as possible be retained in employment until the age of retirement (subject to transfer within the undertaking, where necessary with the appropriate retraining), unless they have, in accordance with collective agreements, national laws or current practice, the possibility of retiring on reasonable terms.

14. Where workers have to be dismissed or laid off because of economic or technological reasons or because of reorganisation, the following measures should be considered, in accordance with national laws, regulations and practices, to mitigate the consequences of such action:

*(a)* the selection of workers to be affected should be made in accordance with precise criteria—determined, in advance wherever possible, after consultation with workers' representatives—such as length of service, competence, family situation and age, and taking into account the need for the efficient operation of the undertaking;

*(b)* a reasonable period of notice should be given to the workers to be affected;

*(c)* provision should be made for appropriate compensation for the workers affected, which could include, for example, unemployment insurance or other forms of social security, or severance allowance or other types of separation benefits paid for by the employer, or a combination of benefits, depending upon national laws or regulations, collective agreements and the personnel policy of the employer;

*(d)* workers whose employment has been terminated owing to a reduction of the workforce should be given priority of re-engagement, to the extent possible, by the employer when he again engages workers; such priority of re-engagement may be limited to a specified period of time;

*(e)* the employer should assist the workers affected to obtain training for alternative employment within the undertaking; the appropriate public authorities should do the same outside the undertaking.

15. Airline companies with activities and personnel employed in countries other than that in which the companies are registered should respect the labour legislation of those countries. In the event of circumstances which might involve collective dismissals or layoffs, reasonable notice of such dismissals or layoffs should be given to the appropriate government authorities and workers' representatives with a view to mitigating hardships for the personnel affected.

## Training

16. Well developed systems of training are essential to employment security in the civil aviation industry where technological change and requirements of high levels of skill are such important factors. Appropriate training systems and facilities, following initial training, are of great importance in order to provide the recurrent training required for personnel to maintain their levels of competence, the transitional training necessary to enable them to qualify for work with new equipment, aircraft or procedures and the training required for redeployment within the industry. Availability of training in administrative skills as well as in other skills is relevant for some of these purposes.

17. Employers, workers and their organisations, the appropriate public authorities and educational and training institutions should co-operate in developing the training systems needed to help safeguard employment security in civil aviation as well as in promoting full utilisation of these training facilities by the personnel concerned, and in particular older personnel.

## International labour standards

18. The Meeting calls on all member States of the International Labour Organisation to apply in civil aviation the principles embodied in the Discrimination (Employment and Occupation) Convention (No. 111) and Recommendation (No. 111) of 1958, and the Termination of Employment Recommendation, 1963 (No. 119).

19. The problems arising with respect to employment security in civil aviation should be borne in mind in any revision of the Termination of Employment Recommendation, 1963 (No. 119).

Conclusions of the Tripartite Technical Meeting for Civil Aviation, 1977

## 3. Security of employment and income in the light of structural changes in the textiles industry

The Textiles Committee of the International Labour Organisation,

Having met in Geneva, in its Eleventh Session, from 10 to 18 October 1984,

Having discussed the report (Report II) on "Security of Employment and Income in the Light of Structural Changes in the Textiles Industry" which had been prepared by the International Labour Office;

Adopts this eighteenth day of October 1984 the following conclusions:

### General considerations

1. Important structural changes are taking place today in the textiles industry in both industrialised and developing countries. In some cases these structural changes have seriously affected employment of textile workers, entailing substantial and lasting reductions in employment in many countries.

2. The causes of structural change vary widely from one country to another. They include technological innovation and changes in the patterns of international trade.

3. For the past decade, structural changes in the textiles industry have occurred in the context of a decline in the rate of economic growth and recession in many countries. This has made adjustments to structural changes and the preservation of employment and income security all the more difficult.

4. Under these circumstances, it is crucially important that vigorous efforts should be made by governments, employers and workers of textile-producing countries to strengthen the viability and competitive vitality of the textiles industry of their respective countries, bearing in mind, in particular, the obligations of the governments concerned to adopt certain social and economic policies under the framework of international trade agreements in textiles to which they are parties.

5. In order to maintain labour standards designed to improve the levels of working and living conditions and to promote sound industrial relations in textile-producing countries, efforts should be made to implement ILO standards, especially the Freedom of Association and Protection of the Right to Organise Convention, 1948 (No. 87), the Right to Organise and Collective Bargaining Convention, 1949 (No. 98), the Equal Remuneration Convention, 1951 (No. 100), the Abolition of Forced Labour Convention, 1957 (No. 105), the Discrimination (Employment and Occupation) Convention, 1958 (No. 111), and the Termination of Employment Convention, 1982 (No. 158), wherever this has not yet been done.

## Information, consultation, negotiation

6. When an enterprise has to take measures to adapt to structural changes, the employer should provide the workers' representatives with information about the situation and consult them about measures to improve the prospects of the undertaking.

7. When, in order to meet the enterprise's difficulties, the employer contemplates the introduction of major changes in production, programme, organisation, structure or technology that may entail substantial changes in jobs and working conditions, or terminations, or both, the employer should consult the workers' representatives as early as possible, so that alternative approaches to the problems of the undertaking can be considered, without precluding the need for negotiating the terms and conditions of such changes.

8. When such changes may entail terminations, all parties should be guided by the provisions of the ILO Termination of Employment Convention (No. 158) and Recommendation (No. 166), 1982.

9. When arrangements for adjustment to structural change include financial and/or other forms of assistance by public authorities at the level of the enterprise, of the industry as a whole, or of certain sections of the industry, the workers' representatives should be informed of and consulted on the means of obtaining such assistance.

10. The purpose of the consultations and any negotiations mentioned in paragraphs 7 and 9 should be to avert or minimise terminations and to mitigate their

effects, without prejudice to the efficient operation of the undertaking, by appropriate methods such as those mentioned in paragraphs 12–23 of this document.

11. Governments should, in accordance with national law and practice, encourage consultations and negotiations as mentioned in paragraphs 6, 7 and 9.

## Measures to enhance employment security at the enterprise level

12. When structural change endangers the continued full operation of the enterprise and some or all of its jobs, the employer and workers have a common interest in attempting to reinforce the undertaking's economic strength as the base of employment security.

13. Such attempts should, to the greatest extent possible, seek to increase the firm's revenue in various ways including, for instance, diversification within or outside the textiles industry or specialisation of its product range. To the extent that these measures are successful, workers should be entitled to a fair share in their results.

14. To the extent that restoring the enterprise's viability depends on cost reduction, the employer and workers have a common interest in improving the undertaking's productivity. The introduction, for this purpose, of new equipment, processes, organisation and conditions of work should provide for information to and consultation with workers' representatives leading, where considered necessary by the parties, to negotiations on the optimum level of employment and income consistent with the continued efficient operation of the undertaking.

15. In order to avert or minimise termination of employment, there should be negotiation, where this is considered necessary by the parties concerned, on all appropriate arrangements of work and working time of workers and machines as well as internal redeployment of personnel, which are compatible with the economic and technological requirements of the enterprise. In this connection, regard should be given to the workers' earnings.

## The role of the public authorities

16. The role of the public authorities in individual countries varies according to their political and social systems, the extent of participation of the public authorities in the ownership of the textiles industry, where such participation exists, and the effectiveness of collective bargaining. A common feature of all cases is that financial or other appropriate intervention by the public authorities should be considered only if its perceived advantages exceed its perceived costs; however, the perception of advantages and costs itself will differ from case to case.

17. Relevant action of the public authorities should normally be taken at the national and industry level, in the light of their responsibilities for overall economic and social policies, including their concern with international trade and their role in fulfilling the objectives of international trade agreements in textiles to which they are parties. At each level of decision, there should be consultation regarding action contemplated by public authorities with appropriate representatives of employers and workers, so that alternative approaches can be attained.

18. In countries whose textiles industry is adversely affected by international competition, action by the public authorities should include measures to encourage enterprises that are less competitive to consider moving into other lines of production or into other sectors of the economy. Government action may also include financial and technical assistance to the restructuring of individual enterprises, especially small- and medium-sized enterprises and, for assistance, to research and development for the benefit of the industry as a whole. However, such aid and assistance should not have the effect of distorting competition.

19. With regard to redundancies arising from structural change, the government should normally provide employment market services to facilitate the re-engagement of workers either within or outside the textile industry and financial aid to facilitate their relocation and retraining if necessary. It may also supplement existing financial benefits for workers with a view to facilitating early retirement, appropriate arrangements of work and working time of workers and unavoidable terminations of employment. Where workers' organisations are weak or non-existent it is particularly important that the government, in accordance with national law and practice, should set minimum standards of employment and income security.

## Workforce reduction

20. When, as a result of structural changes, an enterprise must reduce its workforce, and if termination of employment or temporary lay-offs are inevitable as a means of achieving the workforce reduction, the selection by the employer of workers to be affected by these measures should be made according to criteria established wherever possible in advance, having regard to Paragraph 23 of the ILO Termination of Employment Recommendation, 1982 (No. 166).

21. When an employer contemplates terminations of employment or temporary lay-offs as a means of workforce reduction, he should—

(i) give the workers affected by these measures a reasonable period of notice or compensation in lieu thereof;
(ii) provide the workers' representatives concerned in good time with relevant information including the reasons for the terminations or lay-offs contemplated and the criteria applied for the selection of the workers affected;
(iii) give, in accordance with national law and practice, the workers' representatives concerned, as early as possible, an opportunity for consultation on the application of the criteria mentioned in (ii) above, as well as measures to mitigate the adverse effects of the terminations or lay-offs; and
(iv) notify, in accordance with national law and practice, the competent authority as early as possible, giving relevant information, including a written statement of the reasons for the terminations or lay-offs, the number and categories of workers likely to be affected and the period over which the terminations or lay-offs are intended to be carried out;
(v) assist, if possible and where necessary, the workers affected in the search for suitable alternative employment, for example through direct contacts with other employers.

22. Workers whose employment has been terminated for reasons of an economic, technological, structural or similar nature should in accordance with national law and practice be provided with adequate severance allowances or unemployment benefits or a combination of both, as appropriate.

## Future ILO action

23. The ILO should expand its programme for assistance in the development of small-scale enterprises in developing countries to include strengthening of small-scale enterprises in the textiles industry affected by structural change by way of appropriate management training and development. The ILO should seek to introduce additional systems of monitoring in relation to such programmes.

24. The ILO should also give special attention in its training programmes for developing countries to the needs for improved training methodologies for the training of workers in the textiles industry, the production of training material for this purpose, and assistance in the setting up of training schemes and courses. The services of the ILO's Turin Centre should be used to the fullest extent in such activities. The ILO should seek to introduce additional systems of monitoring in relation to such programmes.

Conclusions of the Textiles Committee, Eleventh Session, 1984

## Remuneration

### 1. Selection, design and administration of appropriate pay systems

#### I. Introduction

1. The term "pay system" is used here to refer to the various rules and procedures established within an enterprise to determine the entitlements of workers to diverse forms of remuneration. The three most prominent pay system issues are the elaboration of appropriate relative pay structures for the various jobs or categories of workers; the establishment, if practicable, of links between pay and performance; the determination of the various components of direct and indirect remuneration entering into the total remuneration package. Pay system practices can have an important bearing on industrial relations, productivity and earnings levels. While pay system reform is not the only, nor necessarily the most important means through which improved job satisfaction, motivation and industrial relations may be achieved, it none the less warrants close attention from the social partners, as with the passage of time pay practices can readily lose their effectiveness.

2. It is desirable to distinguish, to the extent possible, pay system issues from problems of determining overall pay levels. However, in practice, the two types of problems are often closely inter-related. The extent to which an enterprise may have scope for effecting reforms in pay systems depends largely on the general level of wages paid by the enterprise and its economic situation. Enterprises and workers should have regard for the importance of selecting a satisfactory base wage upon which to build a pay system. The introduction of new pay systems should not be used as a device for reducing wages.

3. Pay systems need to be adapted to the context in which they are to operate. They must be specifically designed to compensate and thus to encourage skill acquisition, effort, commitment, adaptation, innovation or other forms of behaviour that are considered most essential for organisational success. At the same time, they must be compatible with the values and attitudes of the workers concerned and take into account the economic, institutional and technological constraints confronting the organisation. Thus, pay systems are most apt to function well when employers and workers within enterprises are able to exercise considerable discretion in selecting and designing systems closely in line with their own needs and are committed to undertaking their regular review.

4. Desired forms of behaviour can be expected to be encouraged through pay systems only when they are well understood and accepted by the workers to whom they are to apply. This underscores the importance of simplicity and transparency in the administration of pay schemes, and of ensuring that such schemes are regarded as equitable. These objectives are more likely to be achieved when workers and/or their representatives play a significant role in the process of pay system design, introduction and application. The methods to be followed in the introduction and application of pay systems should be the subject of early consultation and, wherever possible, collective bargaining between the employers and workers concerned.

5. Pay systems can be expected to function efficiently in the long run only when they are perceived as serving the interests of both workers and employers. Hence pay systems need to include adequate safeguards and joint procedures should be introduced to ensure that they are implemented fairly. The commonality of interests of workers and employers in improved productivity, earnings and equity is likely to be much more apparent where pay systems are developed and elaborated in accordance with rules established through collective bargaining.

## II. Establishing the pay structure

### Basis of the pay structure

6. Structures of relative pay in an enterprise must be both *rational* and *equitable*. They must be rational in the sense that they are adequate to attract and to retain sufficient numbers of staff with the varying skills required by the enterprise, as well as to encourage workers to perform well, to improve their skills and to take up more demanding jobs. At the same time, they must be equitable and the remuneration received by workers must be perceived by them as proportionate to their skills and their contributions to the productive process. Potential conflicts between internal equity and external competitiveness need to be clearly recognised and reconciled in ways best adapted to the circumstances of the enterprise.

7. In the fixing of relative pay, enterprises must decide on the extent to which their structures should be based or the nature of the tasks to be performed, worker skills and other personal characteristics (e.g. aptitudes, levels of education, age and seniority) or a combination of these methods. The choice should reflect technological innovation, prevailing notions of equity and work organisation requirements for the categories of workers and enterprises concerned.

8. The main advantages of pay structures based essentially on workers' skills and/or personal characteristics are their simplicity and the stability and security of pay they afford to workers. They also may permit the employer much flexibility in the distribution of tasks in accordance with individual capacities and changing operational needs. The main disadvantage is that large divergencies can readily emerge between relative pay levels and the difficulty and importance of the tasks actually performed by various workers. Basing pay on occupational qualifications or skill requirements may be suitable where jobs are relatively homogeneous and clearly related to recognised skills for their satisfactory performance and where a finely graded pay structure is not viewed as necessary. Pay structures based on personal characteristics are more apt to be appropriate where workers have a long-term commitment to the enterprise and a strong expectation of a regular career progression; Where individual jobs are difficult to define independently of the contributions made by the persons occupying them, considerable flexibility is required from the workforce, and the existing norms of equity strongly favour personal characteristics as the basis of payment.

9. In most countries and for most sectors and categories of workers, the most widely applicable approach for larger enterprises has been to base pay structures on actual or presumed job content without initially taking into account the individual abilities, characteristics or performance of the workers concerned. Basing relative pay

essentially on the difficulty and importance of the tasks to be performed has the advantage of giving explicit recognition to the principle of equal pay for equal work. Moreover, this approach helps avoid situations where pay is made for worker qualifications not actually required by the organisation. However, in some cases the notion of the job may not always be self-evident or may be hard to distinguish from the personal contributions of individual workers. Also linking pay to specific tasks may impede flexibility in the use of the workforce or skill acquisition.

10. To meet the needs of complex organisations, combined methods of establishing the pay structure should often be followed with compensation being provided not just for job content but also for the types of worker contributions recognised more explicitly in the other approaches such as seniority, versatility and qualifications over and above the minimum requirements for the job. Similarly, it is to be expected that approaches based on qualifications or personal characteristics would often need to be supplemented by allowances or other wage components related to job content. Whatever the approach followed, however, for the structure of pay to be accepted as equitable and rational there must be a close correspondence between the pay received by individual workers and the importance of their contribution to the enterprise. Many distortions in relative pay derive from imbalances between job tasks, worker qualifications and their personal characteristics.

*Job evaluation*

11. Determining the relative position of jobs in a pay hierarchy may be carried out in an informal way based largely on job titles or simple rules of thumb, or it may be the result of formalised procedures, that is job evaluation. The main advantage of job evaluation is that judgements concerning the relative value of jobs are made systematically. Even though this technique cannot be described as "scientific" or "objective", as it rests in the final analysis on personal judgements, these judgements are nevertheless made consistently on the basis of concrete components of the job or through job comparisons. As a result, simple, more readily understandable and explainable pay structures are likely to be established. Grievances over relative pay for existing, new or changed jobs are likely to be reduced or more quickly or satisfactorily resolved. In addition, a basis may be provided from which individual performance may be assessed. Moreover, another essential advantage lies in the fact that in the course of the process of job evaluation, the nature and the volume of the various tasks belonging to various jobs are gauged concretely. This helps to better distribute tasks among the various jobs and to improve work organisation, the structure of departments, and the general management of the enterprise. The information gathered on jobs may be useful in making wage comparisons with other enterprises, in recruitment, selection, training, as well as in transfers and promotions. The main disadvantage of job evaluation is the time and resources needed for its introduction and administration. This may appear disproportionate having regard to the results that might have been expected from less formalised approaches to fixing relative pay, especially in smaller enterprises with a limited range of different jobs, where tasks change frequently or where it is difficult to dissociate the characteristics of the worker from the requirements of the job. Also the bureaucratic procedures associated with job evaluation plans may create much dysfunctional behaviour and

not everyone may be convinced that it is possible or desirable to predetermine the criteria on which jobs should be classified. Another limitation is that although job evaluation may be a useful starting point for bringing about improvements in organisational structures and the distribution of tasks, by itself it cannot achieve this goal and is bound to produce unsatisfactory results unless such deficiencies are rectified.

12. There are a wide variety of job evaluation methods that may be relied upon. Most of these are based on one of the four traditional methods, viz. ranking, classification, point rating and factor comparison, or are hybrids of these methods. The choice among these methods should take into consideration the general nature of the work, the number and complexity of the jobs to be evaluated, the speed and accuracy with which the evaluations have to be made, other possible uses for information generated through the job evaluation process and the views of employees and their representatives. *Ranking*, either made directly or through paired comparisons, is likely to appear more appropriate in smaller organisational units with a limited range of jobs, where speedy and low-cost implementation is important, and where great accuracy, the recording of detailed job information and explanations of classification decisions are not necessary. Job evaluation through *classification* on the basis of predetermined grade definitions is likely to be appropriate where a simple, non-analytical (or non-quantitative) method will suffice, jobs are sufficiently homogeneous that groups can be clearly defined and continuing change in job content is not expected. The *point-rating* method is most likely to be considered appropriate where the need for accuracy, job information and a clear justification for pay decisions makes the extra costs of an analytical method appear worth while, where the need to rank a large number of jobs of quite different kinds makes it essential to consider a series of factors common to them, where job content is likely to undergo continuing modifications and where the expectation is that jobs will ultimately be classified into a relatively large number of different pay grades. The *factor comparison* method is more apt to appear appropriate where an analytical approach is required, substantial costs are willing to be incurred to introduce a system, and where the application of a complex methodology does not generate problems of comprehension or employee acceptance and there is a wish to tie the pay structure closely to the relative rates of benchmark jobs or wages prevailing on the labour market.

13. When selecting a job evaluation method and adapting it to the needs of the enterprise, it needs to be kept in mind that the main objective is not to determine the "value" of jobs in some absolute sense but rather to achieve a consensus among the parties concerned regarding the position of jobs in the enterprise job hierarchy. For this reason, it is increasingly being accepted that worker representatives should be given the opportunity to participate in job evaluation wherever practicable. Worker participation can take the form of participating in decisions with respect to the selection of an appropriate method, the determination of the structure of the plan, the preparation and approval of job descriptions, the evaluation of jobs and the settlement of disputes over grading. It should be stated, however, that the different stages of the application of the scheme are linked, and that workers can assume no responsibility for the results of those stages in which they did not participate.

14. Job evaluation must be based on accurate job information. Even though it may be time consuming, it is necessary to gather information on the tasks and

requirements of each job, relationships among jobs and environmental conditions, and to organise this information in accordance with a standard format that facilitates comparisons. Job analyses involving actual observation of workers at the workplace should be carried out. The job description should be understandable for the workers, and, to ensure its accuracy, should be agreed to by them. The degree of detail to be included in the job descriptions should depend on the method of job evaluation to be used and the other purposes to which the job information may be put. An overly detailed description may limit flexibility in work assignments and prompt too many demands for grading reviews whereas an overly general description may leave too much latitude to judgement.

15. Experience shows that the selection of benchmark jobs is an important step, particularly for non-analytical methods where they serve as points of comparison for the evaluation of other jobs. Wherever possible benchmark jobs should be representative of the totality of jobs being evaluated, well-known and easily defined, and accepted as having a fair relative remuneration.

16. The selection and definition of factors is a critical step in the execution of analytical job evaluation methods. Broad generic factors, such as skill, responsibility, effort and working conditions, should be modified or broken down in different ways so as to make their application as precise as possible for the enterprise and category of workers concerned. The set of factors and sub-factors should be: sufficiently comprehensive to cover all essential aspects of jobs while avoiding overlapping and double counting; limited in number so as to avoid including considerations of only minor significance; present in varying degrees in all the jobs being considered; capable of being clearly defined and divided into varying degree levels that can be easily understood; free from sex bias or other forms of implicit discrimination.

17. In point-rating schemes the weighting of factors should be determined pragmatically in the light of judgements concerning equity, the avoidance of manifest or latent sex discrimination, and the impact on the existing pay structure. Statistical methods may be useful in deriving a suitable weighting pattern but the final test must be its acceptability for everyone concerned.

18. The scope of job evaluation plans has an important bearing on the selection and definition of factors. Plans covering more than the individual enterprise (e.g. industry or national schemes) or several categories of workers (e.g. manual, administrative, technical and supervisory staff) can make a contribution towards eliminating various inequalities or inequities. However, the broader the scope of the scheme, the more difficult it becomes to define precise criteria and to reconcile internal rates with those practised on the labour market.

19. All workers should be supplied with suitable information on the objectives and steps in the job evaluation exercise, and those directly involved should receive suitable training. There should be a possibility for appeals against evaluation decisions and procedures should be established for re-evaluating jobs following changes in tasks or responsibilities.

## III. Linking pay to performance

### Payment by results

20. The term "payment by results" (hereafter PBR) refers to pay systems under which at least a part of workers' earnings vary directly with measured changes in performance in accordance with predetermined rules. The main ways by which PBR schemes can be distinguished are: *(a)* the unit whose performance is measured and compensated (individual workers, small teams or groups of workers, entire departments, divisions, plants or enterprises); *(b)* the nature of the results being measured and compensated (output, quality, process yield, rates of material or machine utilisation, productivity indices, cost ratios, meeting of targets or some combination of these results); *(c)* the period over which results are measured; *(d)* the proportion of expected earnings that is variable; *(e)* the relation between variations in performance and pay.

21. Depending on their characteristics, PBR schemes may be designed to achieve varying goals. Accordingly, scheme objectives need to be carefully formulated taking into account those aspects of performance considered most critical for organisational effectiveness. In doing so, it should be recognised that conflicts may exist between the pursuit of varying objectives. For instance, schemes directed towards stimulating high levels of output may make it more difficult to encourage innovative or co-operative behaviour or may jeopardise the goal of sound industrial relations. Also, schemes that one may expect to make an important contribution to the goal of higher productivity and earnings in the short term may not necessarily do so in the long run.

22. Ideally, the measures of performance to be used in PBR schemes should be as comprehensive as possible because aspects of performance that are measured and rewarded are bound to be pursued at the expense of those that are not. At the same time, the performance being measured should be directly subject to worker control. The extent to which available performance measures meet these two criteria will largely determine the scope, if any, for successfully applying PBR schemes of various types.

### Individual PBR

23. The most frequently identified advantages of well-functioning PBR schemes based on individual output are: *(a)* higher levels of productivity, lower costs of production and increased earnings; *(b)* the need for less supervision; *(c)* more worker choice regarding the pace of work and earnings received; *(d)* labour costs per unit of output subject to more accurate estimation.

24. On the other hand, experience shows that such advantages may be in part or wholly offset by problems such as: *(a)* increased risks to safety and health owing to a faster pace of work or pressures to avoid prescribed work methods; *(b)* difficulties in maintaining quality standards and avoiding wage drift, that is, uncontrolled increases in earnings ahead of negotiated wage changes; *(c)* substantial administrative expenses disproportionate to expected productivity improvements; *(d)* more difficult workflow planning; *(e)* possible adverse effects on morale and time-consuming disputes, owing to unpredictable fluctuations in earnings, differences in earnings

or effort expended by different categories of workers and competition among workers; *(f)* the restriction of output by workers caused by the belief that high earnings will lead to tighter standards or lower increases in basic wages; *(g)* worker resistance to changes in working methods, transfers to new jobs or temporary redeployments, for fear of reduced earnings.

25. Basic factors that should be considered when judging whether individual PBR schemes might be successfully applied to the long-term benefit of both the workers and employers concerned are as follows:

*(a)* *Risks to safety and health.* Individual PBR should not be used where work is inherently hazardous or where there is evidence indicating or reasonable grounds to believe that the greater work intensity associated with individual PBR may result in higher rates of accidents or undue fatigue or stress.

*(b)* *The motivational effectiveness of money.* Individual PBR will be more appropriate where adequate levels of motivation cannot be sustained through other means (e.g. skilled supervision, target-setting, job design) and where workers attach sufficient importance to earning extra money, trust that the scheme will be operated fairly and accept the principle that pay should vary with measured results and the attendant risk that their earnings may fluctuate.

*(c)* *The ease of measurement of results.* Systems of individual PBR require accurate standard setting. This is easier for simple short-cycle manual work that is both repetitive and not subject to important variations from one cycle to the next.

*(d)* *The directness of the relationship between effort and results.* Individual PBR schemes are not likely to work effectively where: the pace of work is beyond worker control; frequent work interruptions occur; quality standards are difficult to meet; and workers are often shifted from one task to another.

*(e)* *The practicality of efficient administrative controls.* Administrative and production systems must be adequate: to limit possible abuses of the pay system; to set and revise accurate standards; to accomodate variations in individual output and to ensure that workers are regularly provided with equitable earning opportunities.

*(f)* *Vulnerability to equity disputes.* Individual PBR schemes may constitute a continuing source of disruptive disputes where: opportunities to earn bonuses cannot be extended to all groups of workers among whom earnings comparisons are traditionally made; divisions in the workforce give rise to invidious earnings comparisons; and the formal and informal procedures for resolving workplace grievances function poorly.

26. Systems of individual PBR should: *(a)* be kept simple so that workers can check their earnings without difficulty; *(b)* lead to an appreciable increase in earnings; *(c)* be based on an equitable structure of hourly rates and accurate standards that incorporate reasonable allowances for fatigue, personal needs and other factors recognised in sound work measurement practice.

27. The most widely used schemes are straight-proportional, that is, earnings above the guaranteed time rate vary in the same proportion as output. Since such schemes are easy for workers to understand, provide a strong incentive for good performance and are more easily accepted as equitable by workers, they should be

given first consideration for adoption. Other forms should be considered only if special circumstances warrant their application. In particular, "stabilised" or regressive schemes in which earnings rise less rapidly than output are generally considered for use only where existing levels of performance are judged to be quite low, work interruptions are relatively frequent, accurate standards are difficult to set and maintain, and quite high levels of output might be harmful.

28. In general, a worker's performance should be measured and compensated over as short a period as possible so that a direct relation is established between effort and earnings. However, on work with exceptionally long-cycle times, which is quite difficult to measure or subject to frequent interruptions, a longer period for performance measurement should be used in order to reduce fluctuations in earnings.

29. Workers should be protected against undue fluctuations in earnings through a time-rate guarantee. Whenever practical, this time-rate guarantee should operate over a reasonable period so that bonuses earned in any given period are not lost through subsequent low production. The variable part of earnings should be large enough to encourage good performance but not so large as to expose workers to significant variations in earnings for reasons beyond their control. Where conditions favouring the successful application of individual PBR are not fully met, a lower portion of variable earnings should be provided for in order to ensure continuing acceptability and to prevent pay system erosion. Often it will prove useful to reach a common prior understanding on the amount of bonus a scheme is designed to yield on average in order to serve as a guide in judging how a scheme is functioning. The earnings guarantee for work interruptions for causes beyond the workers' control should be the time-rate guarantee.

30. To ensure that standards are not tightened simply because earnings are high their modification should occur only for agreed reasons such as changes in work content, methods of production or the correction of clerical errors, or when agreed upon by the workers and their representatives.

31. Rules for the conduct of work measurement studies should be prescribed in advance and, where possible, through joint agreement. Concealed studies should be prohibited and workers or their representatives notified in advance when studies are to be undertaken. New standards should be subject to challenge through an established appeal procedure that ensures a speedy resolution of the issue. When challenges are raised, all relevant information on how standards have been established should be provided and reviews made of the original studies as necessary. Provision should be made for the participation of workers' representatives in the standard-setting process in a manner to be defined by collective agreements. Such participation might involve collaboration in the conduct of time studies, consultations on who is to be timed, consultations or negotiations on the introduction of new standards and/or participation in the review bodies established to deal with appeals.

32. Appropriate measures should be agreed in advance between management and the workers' representatives to provide for workers who may become redundant as a result of the introduction of the scheme. These measures if agreed could include, in priority, transfers to other jobs where available or justifiable given the economic circumstances of the enterprise, or severance arrangements. The method of operation of the schemes must be carefully explained to all those who will be affected by them. The principles underlying the scheme, the workers to be covered, earnings guarantees,

other safeguards and all the facts relevant to a scheme's operation should be elaborated in a document that is generally available to workers and their representatives.

## Group PBR

33. The main advantage of group as opposed to individual output-related PBR schemes is that compensation is provided for co-operative behaviour among the group members. This should encourage them to minimise idle time and unnecessary absenteeism, to aid colleagues clear bottlenecks and backlogs, to pay more attention to the quality of products that will be handled by other group members, to be more adaptable in accommodating production alterations, and to be more flexible in accepting changes in work methods and job assignments. Group payment can also facilitate improvements in work organisation and is less likely to entail risks to safety and health. The processes of pay system erosion and wage drift are more easily avoided and pay disputes are likely to be reduced since earnings are more stable and uniform within the group and standards more readily controllable. Administrative costs are lower since standard-setting is easier, record keeping simplified and supervisory costs reduced since the points at which quality inspections need to be carried out can be fewer and less time needs to be spent in administering the pay system. Finally the induction training of new group members is likely to be facilitated by other group members.

34. The main disadvantage of group PBR is that the less direct relation between individual pay and performance may cause effort levels to slacken compared with what they might be under individual PBR, particularly for better performers. Moreover, conflict within the group may arise if the better performers are convinced that not everyone is making a fair contribution to the common goal.

35. Group payment is applicable where jobs are interdependent either because they are performed in sequence, as in assembly line work, or joint efforts are required to ensure good performance. Group payment is also appropriate where work group pressures are exceptionally strong and favour equality of earnings. The greater the cohesiveness of the group in terms of social compatibility, levels of skill, physical proximity and community of interest, the more likely that group norms will favour group payment. Group payment should also be relied upon where it would be impractical to measure individual output with sufficient accuracy to make individual PBR viable; where it is important to include in the scheme aspects of performance that are only measurable at the group level; where the frequency of changes in production processes or work interruptions make it necessary to encourage flexible and adaptable behaviour or perhaps a shift toward group work production arrangements; and where individual payment would risk causing many disruptive disputes.

36. Although most aspects of design, introduction and administration are similar for both individual and group PBR schemes, some special problems exist: *(a)* everything else being equal, it is better to maintain group size as small as possible so that the relation between effort and results remains as direct as possible; *(b)* groups should also be relatively homogeneous in terms of performance and well integrated both by the nature of the jobs and socially; *(c)* groups should be kept as stable as possible, since new members will naturally, for a period of time, produce less than the

experienced members (as necessary, special allowances for new members or young or older workers should be made so that the effects on group earnings are minimised); *(d)* whatever method is selected for distribution of bonus earnings among group members should be consistent with group member views regarding contributions to the group results.

## *Plant or enterprise PBR*

37. By relying on quite broad measures of performance these schemes aim to achieve a greater convergence between the overall goals of the organisation and those of the individual worker and more effective collaboration amongst various categories of workers and functional units. The emphasis is essentially on encouraging more innovative and adaptive co-operative behaviour in the most effective utilisation of all the organisation's resources. Workers are encouraged to suggest cost-saving changes, to co-operate with each other and management in the sharing of knowledge, to help each other as the need arises, and to accept more readily flexibility in work assignments and technological and organisational changes. At the same time, workers are likely to be less tolerant of poor planning, over-manning, idle time, restrictions on output, and poor quality work. Workers' morale and job satisfaction may be improved as a result of mutually reinforcing group behaviour and more opportunity to participate in the affairs of the enterprise. Additional practical advantages are more ready availability of comprehensive performance measures, quick installations and low administrative costs, and comparatively easy control.

38. The main disadvantage is that only a remote relation may be perceived between individual worker efforts and bonus earnings. In addition, the performance measure, beside often being difficult to understand, is in many cases subject to major variations for reasons clearly beyond the workers' and management control.

39. Enterprise or plant level schemes are likely to prove most successful where: *(a)* the unit of accountability is comparatively small so that there are close personal contacts between workers and managers, the definition of an appropriate performance measure does not become too complex, and some relation can be perceived between improvements made and bonus received; *(b)* it is evident to everyone concerned that the organisation's success depends on continuing adaptation, team work and co-operative behaviour, and that the scope for improving productivity or reducing costs is not likely to fall off quickly with time; *(c)* one can define a measure of performance that is simple and readily calculated at frequent intervals, yet to a large degree controllable by the efforts of the workforce; *(d)* the product mix and production arrangements are sufficiently stable to reduce the frequency of having to renegotiate the performance standard; *(e)* management is able to communicate effectively, receptive to new ideas coming from workers and willing to devote the time necessary to administer the scheme; *(f)* employees are technically knowledgeable, interested in participating in decisions and committed on a long-term basis to the organisation; *(g)* there is a high level of trust in the organisation and trade unions fully endorse the scheme and do not perceive it as a threat to their right to defend their members' interests through collective bargaining.

40. Schemes of this type function most effectively when they are accompanied by a formal participative system that facilitates: *(a)* the transformation of agreed

practical suggestions into actual changes in operating methods and procedures; *(b)* two-way communications at all levels on operating difficulties and general business trends; *(c)* direct worker involvement in pay system procedures so that employees may be confident that bonuses are being determined fairly.

### *Time-rate systems*

41. As the conditions for the successful application of PBR schemes are quite stringent, it is to be expected that in most countries most workers would continue to be paid exclusively or essentially on a time-rate basis. Administrative simplicity, strong worker preference for fixed payment, reduced scope for disputes over pay equity and the adequacy of non-financial approaches to sustaining adequate levels of motivation are frequently decisive factors favouring the use of time-rate systems. However, through the use of measured daywork and merit rating, it may be possible in some instances to incorporate into time-rate systems some of the advantages of maintaining an explicit link between pay and performance.

## IV. Developing the pay package

42. It is advisable whenever necessary to review the varying components of direct pay to ensure that they remain well-integrated into a rational structure of direct cash compensation. In particular, forms of payment should be simplified and those no longer serving their original purpose should be incorporated into basic wages if that is to the benefit of both workers and employers. Payments that undermine the perceived equity of relative pay should be revised. A well-integrated structure is more easily maintained when basic wages account for a major proportion of direct pay.

43. In addition to direct pay, workers will normally receive various benefits granted at the level of the enterprise. These may be the result of decisions taken at this level or at higher levels. All such benefits, apart from direct pay, received by workers from their employers by virtue of their contract of employment and for which an economic value for the employee can be calculated with reasonable accuracy, should be considered as part of indirect remuneration.

44. Such forms of indirect remuneration should be viewed as serving a variety of purposes. Employer interests in providing indirect remuneration may include the recruitment, retention, welfare and motivation of the workforce, the improvement of productivity, the reduction of labour turnover, the development of greater commitment to enterprise goals and the meeting of social responsibilities to the community. Worker interests in indirect remuneration include essentially greater economic security, but also more convenient purchasing arrangements, and more favourable prices and tax treatment. While some benefits serve employer interests and others the interests of workers, there are many benefits that improve both workers' welfare and enterprise efficiency. In the elaboration of a total remuneration package, the aim should be to meet the interests of both sides to the greatest extent possible.

45. A more appropriate package of total remuneration is likely to emerge when: *(a)* indirect remuneration is regarded as complementary to direct pay and its goals are explicitly formulated; *(b)* the costs of benefits, in terms of their direct pay

equivalent, are specified as precisely as possibly; *(c)* responsibility for benefit planning is clearly established and periodic analysis of benefits is undertaken to assess the adequacy of coverage, overall balance and effectiveness in meeting objectives; *(d)* general practices in the community and workers' attitudes to benefits are ascertained; *(e)* trade unions or other workers' representatives are involved in identifying and representing workers' preferences.

46. Indirect remuneration will not meet its goals unless workers fully understand and appreciate the benefits being provided to them.

47. To increase the value of benefits granted at the enterprise level and awareness of their economic role, wherever and to the extent practicable, workers should be given some choice in selecting the benefits they receive, within the framework of agreed rules established through collective bargaining wherever possible.

48. Although there may be some advantage to establishing different benefit programmes in line with the needs of different categories of workers, there is a danger that these differences may be perceived as unjustly accentuating inequalities in relative pay or as perpetuating unfair treatment based on occupational distinctions. Any differences between categories of workers in access to benefits should have an apparent and generally accepted justification. They should be kept to a minimum, if not entirely eliminated.

49. Benefits once granted by employers on a regular basis should be treated as an integral part of the remuneration package that cannot be removed at will. If such benefits are to be removed because they are no longer useful, they should be discussed through collective bargaining procedures and settled accordingly.

Guidelines adopted by the Meeting of Experts on Pay Systems, 1983

## 2. Methods of wage determination in the postal and telecommunications sector

The Joint Committee for Postal and Telecommunications Services,

Having met in Geneva, in its First Session, from 27 November to 5 December 1984,

Having examined the report presented to it by the International Labour Office on methods of wage determination in the postal and telecommunications sector;

Adopts this fifth day of December 1984 the following conclusions:

### *General considerations*

1. Postal and telecommunications services are an indispensable element in the economic structure; they contribute vitally to the efficiency and development of industry, commerce and other services.

2. They are major employers of labour and their expansion has a multiplier effect on general levels of employment because of their crucial place in the economy.

3. Good communications services also confer personal and social benefits on users in the form of reduced transportation costs, better social contacts and a higher quality of life.

4. Despite recent changes in the structure of postal and telecommunications services in a number of countries, they generally continue to be considered as public services, the aim of which is to provide, at a reasonable cost, reliable and efficient communications to all sections of the population in all regions of the country.

5. Given that postal and telecommunications services often form part of the community services which fall within the public sector, wages and conditions of employment will often (and specially where there is a monopoly) be subject to the same procedures and arrangements as the rest of the public sector.

6. Given the importance and nature of postal and telecommunications services, governments have a special interest in these services, whether they be private or public. It must, however, be recognised that if postal and telecommunications services are to function efficiently and to adapt to the many changes currently taking place, they must be able to pursue policies which will enable them to attract and retain sufficient and appropriately qualified workers. Success in attaining this objective will, to a great extent, be determined by the ability of postal and telecommunications undertakings to ensure that the wages and conditions of employment are perceived as serving the interests of both workers and employers and are such as to attract and retain appropriate staff.

7. Special regulations may be determined by national law or practice for the implementation of these conclusions for the postal and telecommunications administrations.

8. It would assist in staffing postal and telecommunications undertakings if there is the necessary authority to allow management and trade unions representing workers in the sector to determine wages by collective bargaining.

## Institutional procedures for wage determination

9. It is noted that the wages of a large number of postal and telecommunications employees are determined through collective bargaining but that there are some who are denied this right.

10. It is desirable that all postal and telecommunications workers, without distinction, should, through their trade unions, have the right to collective bargaining with regard to the determination of wages.

11. The Joint Committee notes the relevant provisions of ILO Conventions Nos. 98, 151 and 154 and Recommendation No. 163. Governments should take measures to encourage and promote the full development of machinery for collective bargaining between employers and trade unions with a view to the regulation of terms and conditions of employment by means of collective agreements.

12. Although the procedures for bargaining collectively may differ from one country to another, it is advisable that these procedures be negotiated and agreed to with the trade unions concerned.

13. In countries where collective bargaining leading to the determination of wages of postal and telecommunications workers takes place at different levels, the

parties concerned should ensure that there is co-ordination between the levels and that postal and telecommunications trade unions and management are represented at these different levels.

14. Collective bargaining should aim to achieve collective agreements on wages which can be implemented promptly and fully by the authorities concerned.

15. Procedures for the determination of wages and other conditions of employment and for the settlement of disputes should be the subject of collective bargaining between the employers and the trade unions. Provision should also be made for the settlement of disputes through independent and impartial machinery such as mediation, conciliation and voluntary arbitration, established in such a manner as to ensure the confidence of the parties involved. Decisions of these bodies should be fully and promptly implemented.

16. This machinery should be conceived in such a way as to contribute to the promotion of collective bargaining and must not serve as a substitute for, or hinder normal collective bargaining.

## Determination of wage levels

17. In recent years workers in some countries, including postal and telecommunications workers, have experienced a stagnation or decline in real pay. Frequently, this has been a result, not of the economic situation of the sectors involved, but of the pay policies and austerity measures taken by governments.

18. When national pay restraint policies are applied, postal and telecommunications workers should not be singled out for harsher treatment than other categories of workers.

19. In this respect, it must be recalled that the ILO Committee on Freedom of Association has insisted that any pay restraint policy should apply for a limited period only and be accompanied by appropriate safeguards. Moreover, such pay policies, if imposed arbitrarily by governments, clearly constitute a violation of the principle of free collective bargaining.

20. It is clear that levels of pay in postal and telecommunications services will be determined in relation to a number of factors including, for example, comparison with similar jobs in other sectors, changes in the cost of living, the ability of the enterprise or undertaking to pay, changes in productivity, skills and qualifications required, etc.

21. The weight given to these diverse factors will depend upon the traditions and circumstances in different countries. It is, however, in the interests of the services, the employers and the workers in the sector for levels of remuneration to be fair and appropriate. To this end, certain principles must be followed with regard to the determination of levels of remuneration provided by the employer:

*(a)* All elements of remuneration must be open to periodic review and adjustment on the basis of collective bargaining with the trade unions concerned.

*(b)* Changes in elements of remuneration must be the subject of collective bargaining with the trade unions concerned.

*(c)* There should be no discrimination. All postal and telecommunications employees should receive equal remuneration for work of equal value.

*(d)* Where comparability is an element in determining remuneration of postal and telecommunications employees, the methodology used for making comparisons should be clearly understood and established in such a way as to ensure the confidence of the parties involved. Relevant data should be equally available to both partners in negotiations. Where systems of comparison have been agreed with trade unions, they should only be changed or suspended following negotiations with the trade unions concerned.

*(e)* Trade unions must be given access to all information regarding the financial situation of the enterprise or administration which is considered necessary for collective bargaining on levels of wages and remuneration and which is permitted under the rules relating to public or private undertakings.

*(f)* Where important elements of remuneration are dependent upon changes in output or in productivity, whether due to the introduction of new technology or reorganisation of work, it is essential that the methods of measuring output or productivity should be clear, compatible with the concept of public service and, where possible, agreed with the trade unions concerned and that the payments linked to output or productivity should be subject to collective bargaining with the unions concerned.

22. The remuneration of part-time postal and telecommunications workers should also be established in accordance with the principles mentioned above.

23. Rapid technological changes being introduced in postal and telecommunications services often require workers to adapt to new situations through retraining or the acquiring of new skills. It is important that grading and pay structures should be flexible enough to recognise this. In addition, the pay, conditions and acquired rights of any workers affected by these changes should be the subject of collective bargaining.

## Structure and composition of remuneration

24. The major factor determining the remuneration of individual postal and telecommunications workers is the pay and grading structures which exist in most postal and telecommunications undertakings. Pay and grading structures should be so designed as to reflect the staffing needs of the postal and telecommunications sector, encourage the retention of existing staff and offer reasonable opportunities for progression and promotion.

25. Seniority is in some countries an important factor influencing progression within given grades or categories, and promotion. Where promotion is based on individual merit, and where qualifications and merit are equal, seniority should prevail. The systems and methods of appraisal should be the subject of collective bargaining with the trade unions concerned.

26. It is advisable, in the light of technical and other changes taking place, that classification systems should be regularly reviewed in consultation with the unions concerned and any changes in the systems should be the subject of collective bargaining.

27. Wherever job evaluation systems are employed in order to review grading structures, the system to be used and the results of group evaluation exercises should be the subject of collective bargaining with the trade unions.

28. According to the ILO Report, the principle of equal pay for men and women is recognised by postal and telecommunications services in many countries. A particular problem arises, however, when a large proportion of employees are women and when they are concentrated in certain jobs or categories. When reviewing pay and grading structures it is, therefore, essential, if the principle of equal pay for work of equal value is to be fully implemented, to ensure that the jobs predominantly occupied by women are not systematically undervalued.

29. Although the grading structures and the associated pay scales agreed in postal and telecommunications services will be the main influence on the remuneration received by postal and telecommunications employees, other bonuses, payments and allowances related to specific duties or conditions of work or to the cost of living, either generally or in different localities, can form a part of total remuneration.

30. If the purposes of grading systems and pay scales are not to be undermined, it is advisable that other elements of remuneration be periodically reviewed. Wherever appropriate and possible, such payments should be consolidated into the normal pay scales.

Conclusions of the Joint Committee for Postal and Telecommunications Services, First Session, 1984

## Multinational enterprises

### 1. Multinational enterprises and social policy (extract)

[...]

#### Security of employment

24. Governments should carefully study the impact of multinational enterprises on employment in different industrial sectors. Governments, as well as multinational enterprises themselves, in all countries should take suitable measures to deal with the employment and labour market impacts of the operations of multinational enterprises.

25. Multinational enterprises equally with national enterprises, through active manpower planning, should endeavour to provide stable employment for their employees and should observe freely negotiated obligations concerning employment stability and social security. In view of the flexibility which multinational enterprises may have, they should strive to assume a leading role in promoting security of employment, particularly in countries where the discontinuation of operations is likely to accentuate long-term unemployment.

26. In considering changes in operations (including those resulting from mergers, take-overs or transfers of production) which would have major employment effects, multinational enterprises should provide reasonable notice of such changes to the appropriate government authorities and representatives of the workers in their employment and their organisations so that the implications may be examined jointly in order to mitigate adverse effects to the greatest possible extent. This is particularly important in the case of the closure of an entity involving collective lay-offs or dismissals.

27. Arbitrary dismissal procedures should be avoided.

28. Governments, in co-operation with multinational as well as national enterprises, should provide some form of income protection for workers whose employment has been terminated.

[...]

#### Conditions of work and life

##### Wages, benefits and conditions of work

33. Wages, benefits and conditions of work offered by multinational enterprises should be not less favourable to the workers than those offered by comparable employers in the country concerned.

34. When multinational enterprises operate in developing countries, where comparable employers may not exist, they should provide the best possible wages, benefits and conditions of work, within the framework of government policies. These should be related to the economic position of the enterprise, but should be at least adequate to satisfy basic needs of the workers and their families. Where they provide

workers with basic amenities such as housing, medical care or food, these amenities should be of a good standard.

[...]

## Industrial relations

40. Multinational enterprises should observe standards of industrial relations not less favourable than those observed by comparable employers in the country concerned.

### *Freedom of association and the right to organise*

41. Workers employed by multinational enterprises as well as those employed by national enterprises should, without distinction whatsoever, have the right to establish and, subject only to the rules of the organisation concerned, to join organisations of their own choosing without previous authorisation. They should also enjoy adequate protection against acts of anti-union discrimination in respect of their employment.

42. Organisations representing multinational enterprises or the workers in their employment should enjoy adequate protection against any acts of interference by each other or each other's agents or members in their establishment, functioning or administration.

43. Where appropriate, in the local circumstances, multinational enterprises should support representative employers' organisations.

44. Governments, where they do not already do so, are urged to apply the principles of Convention No. 87, Article 5, in view of the importance, in relation to multinational enterprises, of permitting organisations representing such enterprises or the workers in their employment to affiliate with international organisations of employers and workers of their own choosing.

45. Where governments of host countries offer special incentives to attract foreign investment, these incentives should not include any limitation of the workers' freedom of association or the right to organise and bargain collectively.

46. Representatives of the workers in multinational enterprises should not be hindered from meeting for consultation and exchange of view among themselves, provided that the functioning of the operations of the enterprise and the normal procedures which govern relationships with representatives of the workers and their organisations are not thereby prejudiced.

47. Governments should not restrict the entry of representatives of employers' and workers' organisations who come from other countries at the invitation of the local or national organisations concerned for the purpose of consultation on matters of mutual concern, solely on the grounds that they seek entry in that capacity.

### *Collective bargaining*

48. Workers employed by multinational enterprises should have the right, in accordance with national law and practice, to have representative organisations of their own choosing recognised for the purpose of collective bargaining.

49. Measures appropriate to national conditions should be taken, where necessary, to encourage and promote the full development and utilisation of machinery for voluntary negotiation between employers or employers' organisations and workers' organisations, with a view to the regulation of terms and conditions of employment by means of collective agreements.

50. Multinational enterprises, as well as national enterprises, should provide workers' representatives with such facilities as may be necessary to assist in the development of effective collective agreements.

51. Multinational enterprises should enable duly authorised representatives of the workers in their employment in each of the countries in which they operate to conduct negotiations with representatives of management who are authorised to take decisions on the matters under negotiation.

52. Multinational enterprises, in the context of bona fide negotiations with the workers' representatives on conditions of employment, or while workers are exercising the right to organise, should not threaten to utilise a capacity to transfer the whole or part of an operating unit from the country concerned in order to influence unfairly those negotiations or to hinder the exercise of the right to organise; nor should they transfer workers from affiliates in foreign countries with a view to undermining bona fide negotiations with the workers' representatives or the workers' exercise of their right to organise.

53. Collective agreements should include provisions for the settlement of disputes arising over their interpretation and application and for ensuring mutually respected rights and responsibilities.

54. Multinational enterprises should provide workers' representatives with information required for meaningful negotiations with the entity involved and, where this accords with local law and practices, should also provide information to enable them to obtain a true and fair view of the performance of the entity or, where appropriate, of the enterprise as a whole.

55. Governments should supply to the representatives of workers' organisations on request, where law and practice so permit, information on the industries in which the enterprise operates, which would help in laying down objective criteria in the collective bargaining process. In this context, multinational as well as national enterprises should respond constructively to requests by governments for relevant information on their operations.

*Consultation*

56. In multinational as well as in national enterprises, systems devised by mutual agreement between employers and workers and their representatives should provide, in accordance with national law and practice, for regular consultation on matters of mutual concern. Such consultation should not be a substitute for collective bargaining.

*Examination of grievances*

57. Multinational as well as national enterprises should respect the right of the workers whom they employ to have all their grievances processed in a manner consistent with the following provision: any worker who, acting individually or

jointly with other workers, considers that he has grounds for a grievance should have the right to submit such grievance without suffering any prejudice whatsoever as a result, and to have such grievance examined pursuant to an appropriate procedure. This is particularly important whenever the multinational enterprises operate in countries which do not abide by the principles of ILO Conventions pertaining to freedom of association, to the right to organise and bargain collectively and to forced labour.

## Settlement of industrial disputes

58. Multinational as well as national enterprises jointly with the representatives and organisations of the workers whom they employ should seek to establish voluntary conciliation machinery, appropriate to national conditions, which may include provisions for voluntary arbitration, to assist in the prevention and settlement of industrial disputes between employers and workers. The voluntary conciliation machinery should include equal representation of employers and workers.

Triparite Declaration of Principles adopted by the Governing Body of the ILO, 204th Session, 1977

# Annex 1. Documents published in Labour-Management Relations Series, No. 44 which were not reproduced in the present issue

## I. International labour Recommendations

1. Recommendation No. 119 concerning Termination of Employment at the Initiative of the Employer, 1963

## II. Resolutions adopted by the International Labour Conference

1. Resolution concerning the Independence of the Trade Union Movement, 1952
2. Resolution concerning Consultation and Co-operation between Employers and Workers at the Level of the Undertaking, 1952
3. Resolution concerning Labour-Management Relations, 1955
4. Resolution concerning the Protection of Trade Union Rights, 1955
5. Resolution concerning the Abolition of Anti-Trade Union Legislation in the States Members of the International Labour Organisation, 1957
6. Resolution concerning Labour-Management Relations, 1958
7. Resolution concerning Freedom of Association and the Protection of the Right to Organise, Including the Protection of Representatives of Trade Unions at All Levels, 1961
8. Resolution concerning the Promotion of Good Industrial Relations, Particularly in Countries in Course of Development, and Consultation of Employers' and Workers' Organisations, 1962
9. Resolution concerning the concept of Democratic Decision-Making in Programming and Planning for Economic and Social Development, 1964
10. Resolution concerning Freedom of Association, 1964
11. Resolution concerning Workers' Participation in Undertakings, 1966
12. Resolution concerning Action by the International Labour Organisation in the Field of Human Rights and in Particular with Respect to Freedom of Association, 1968
13. Resolution concerning Industrial Relations in the Shipping Industry, 1970
14. Resolution concerning the Social Problems Raised by Multinational Undertakings, 1971
15. Resolution concerning Conditions and Equality of Treatment of Migrant Workers, 1972

## III. Observations adopted by the International Labour Conference

Observations regarding Consultation and Co-operation between Public Authorities and Employers' and Workers' Organisations at the Industrial and National Levels, 1960

## IV. Resolutions, conclusions and declarations adopted by regional conferences

### Conferences of American States Members of the ILO

1. Mexico Resolution concerning Constitutional Provisions for Freedom of Association, 1946
2. Mexico Resolution concerning Freedom of Association, 1946
3. Mexico Resolution concerning Protection of the Right to Organise and to Bargain Collectively, 1946
4. Mexico Resolution concerning the Validity of Collective Agreements, 1946
5. Mexico Resolution concerning the Extension of Collective Agreements, 1946
6. Mexico Resolution concerning Voluntary Conciliation and Arbitration, 1946
7. Mexico Resolution concerning the Organisation of National Labour Conferences, 1946
8. Montevideo Resolution concerning Freedom of Association, 1949
9. Montevideo Resolution concerning the Settlement of Disputes Arising Out of the Interpretation or Application of Collective Agreements, 1949
10. Montevideo Resolution concerning Labour Courts, 1949
11. Petropolis Resolution concerning Freedom of Association, 1952
12. Havana Resolution on Defence of Trade Union Rights, 1956
13. Havana Resolution concerning the Role of Employers and Workers in Programmes to Raise Productivity, 1956
14. Havana Resolution concerning International Action Related to the Role of Employers and Workers in Programmes to Raise Productivity, 1956
15. Havana Resolution concerning the Future Programme of Action of the ILO in the Field of Labour Management Relations, 1956
16. Declaration of Buenos Aires, 1961
17. Buenos Aires Resolution concerning Social Policy and Economic Development, 1961
18. Buenos Aires Resolution concerning the ILO's Programme of Action in the Field of Labour-Management Relations, 1961
19. Caracas Resolution concerning Social Participation in the Development Process, 1970
20. Caracas Resolution concerning Action by the ILO in the Field of Social Participation in the Development Process, 1970
21. Caracas Resolution concerning Remuneration, 1970
22. Caracas Resolution concerning Conditions of Work and Life, 1970

## Regional meeting for the Near and Middle East

Istanbul Resolution on Labour Policy, 1947

## Asian Regional Conferences

1. New Delhi Resolution concerning Tripartite Organisation and Other Appropriate Arrangements, 1947
2. Tokyo Resolution concerning Wages, 1953
3. New Delhi Resolution concerning the Participation of Trade Unions and Employers' Organisations of Asian Countries in the Elaboration and Implementation of Economic Development Programmes, 1957
4. Melbourne Resolution, 1962
5. Observations regarding Government Services for the Improvement of Labour-Management Relations and Settlement of Disputes, 1962
6. Resolution concerning Management Development, with Special Reference to Personnel Policies and Practices, 1968
7. Resolution concerning Freedom of Association in Asia, 1968
8. Resolution concerning Freedom of Association for Workers' and Employers' Organisations and Their Role in Social and Economic Development, 1971

## European Regional Conference

Resolution concerning the Role of Employers and Workers in Programmes to Raise Productivity, 1955

## African Regional Conferences

1. Lagos Resolution concerning Freedom of Association and Protection of the Right to Organise, 1960
2. Lagos Conclusions on Collective Bargaining and Joint Consultation, 1960
3. Addis Ababa Resolution concerning Wage Policy, 1964

# V. Resolutions, conclusions, declarations, memoranda and reports adopted by Industrial Committees and analogous bodies

## Inland Transport Committee

1. Resolution on Industrial Relations, 1947
2. Resolution concerning Technical Methods of Selection of Workers for the Inland Transport Industry, 1949
3. Resolution concerning Methods of Improving Organisation of Work and Output in Ports, 1957

4. Conclusions concerning General Conditions of Work of Railwaymen, 1961
5. Conclusions concerning Social Consequences of Changing Methods and Techniques in Railways and Road Transport, 1961
6. Resolution concerning Freedom of Association in Essential Transport Services, 1961
7. Conclusions concerning Methods of Collective Bargaining and Settlement of Labour Disputes in Rail Transport, 1966
8. Resolution concerning Future Action by the International Labour Organisation in the Field of Transport, 1972

## Coal Mines Committee

1. Statement concerning Labour-Management Relations in the Coal-Mining Industry, 1959
2. Conclusions concerning Problems of Employment Security and Social and Working Conditions for Persons Employed in the Coal-Mining Industry in Periods of Recession in that Industry, 1970

## Iron and Steel Committee

1. Resolution concerning Special Safety Services and Joint Committee, 1946
2. Resolution concerning Collective Bargaining and the Observance of Collective Agreements, 1946
3. Resolution concerning Co-operation at the Industry Level, 1947
4. Resolution concerning Works Committees in the Iron and Steel Industry, 1947
5. Report of the Subcommittee on Human Relations, 1954
6. Memorandum concerning Conditions of Work and Social Problems in the Iron and Steel Industry in Countries in the Course of Industrialisation, 1957
7. Conclusions concerning the Scope and Methods of Collective Bargaining in the Iron and Steel Industry, 1963
8. Conclusions concerning the Role of Employers' and Workers' Organisations in Programming and Planning in the Iron and Steel Industry, 1969
9. Conclusions concerning Wage Protection and Income Security for Workers in the Iron and Steel Industry, 1969
10. Resolution concerning Freedom of Association in the Iron and Steel Industry, 1969

## Metal Trades Committee

1. Consolidated Text of Conclusions and Resolutions Adopted by the Metal Trades Committee at Its Previous Sessions, 1965
2. Conclusions concerning the Role of Employers' and Workers' Organisations in Programming and Planning in the Metal Trades, 1965
3. Resolution concerning Freedom of Association and Trade Union Rights in the Metal Trades, 1965
4. Resolution concerning Multinational Corporations, 1971

STANDARDS AND GUIDING PRINCIPLES

## Textiles Committee

1. Memorandum concerning Labour-Management Relations in Textile Factories, 1955
2. Resolution concerning the Effects of Technological Development in the Textile Industry, 1958
3. Conclusions concerning Structural and Technological Changes in the Textile Industry, 1968
4. Resolution concerning Freedom of Association in the Textile Industry, 1968
5. Resolution concerning the Future Programme of the International Labour Organisation in the Field of the Textile Industry, 1973
6. Resolution concerning a Programme of Research on Multinational Enterprises in the Textile Industry, 1973

## Petroleum Committee

1. Resolution concerning Promotion in the Petroleum Industry, 1947
2. Statement concerning Industrial Relations in the Petroleum Industry, 1948
3. Memorandum on Consultation and Co-operation Within the Undertaking, 1948
4. Resolution concerning Training in Human Relations for Management and Workers, 1948
5. Resolution concerning Conditions of Employment of Contract Labour in the Petroleum industry, 1956
6. Memorandum concerning Human Relations in the Petroleum Industry, 1956
7. Conclusions concerning Trade Union Organisation in the Petroleum Industry, 1960
8. Conclusions concerning Employer-Employee Communication in the Petroleum Industry, 1960
9. Resolution concerning Freedom of Association in the Petroleum Industry, 1966

## Building, Civil Engineering and Public Works Committee

1. Resolution concerning General Principles on Industrial Relations, 1946
2. Resolution concerning Industrial Peace, 1946
3. Resolution concerning Collaboration in the Construction Industries, 1946
4. Resolution concerning the Establishment of National Committees in the Construction Industries, 1946
5. Resolution concerning the General Principles of Industrial Relations, 1949
6. Resolution concerning Labour-Management Co-operation, 1949
7. Resolution concerning the Establishment of a Satisfactory Psychological Climate at the Workplace, 1953
8. Conclusions concerning Young Workers in the Construction Industry, 1959

## Chemical Industries Committee

1. Resolution concerning Industrial Relations in the Chemical Industries, 1958
2. Conclusions concerning the Effects of Advanced Technology on Employment and Conditions of Work in the Chemical Industries, 1969

## Committee on Work on Plantations

1. Resolution concerning Industrial Relations, 1950
2. Conclusions concerning Living and Working Conditions and Productivity on Plantations, 1955
3. Conclusions concerning Practical Measures to Promote Good Labour-Management Relations on Plantations, 1966
4. Conclusions concerning Social Consequences of Technological Development on Plantations, 1971
5. Resolution concerning the Future Work of the International Labour Organisation in Respect of Plantations, 1971
6. Resolution concerning Freedom of Association and the Exercise of Trade Union Rights on Plantations, 1971

## Advisory Committee on Salaried Employees and Professional Workers

1. Resolution concerning Non-Manual Workers and Collective Bargaining, 1957
2. Conclusions concerning Effects of Mechanisation and Automation in Offices, 1959
3. Conclusions concerning the Impact of Social and Economic Developments on Working and Living Conditions in the Distributive Trades, 1967

## Ad Hoc Civil Aviation Meeting

Resolution concerning Joint Consultation in the Civil Aviation Industry, 1960

## Tripartite Technical Meeting on Mines Other than Coal Mines

1. Resolution concerning Machinery for Wage Fixing and Wage Protection in Mines Other than Coal Mines, 1957
2. Memorandum concerning Industrial Relations in Mines Other than Coal Mines, 1957
3. Resolution concerning Freedom of Association and Trade Union Rights in Mines Other than Coal Mines, 1968

## Tripartite Technical Meeting on the Timber Industry

1. Memorandum concerning Labour-Management Relations in the Timber Industry, 1958
2. Resolution concerning Multinational Corporations in the Timber Industry, 1973

## Tripartite Technical Meeting for the Leather and Footwear Industry

Resolution concerning Freedom of Association in the Leather and Footwear Industry, 1969

## Joint Committee on the Public Service

1. Resolution concerning Freedom of Association and Procedures for Staff Participation in Determining Conditions of Employment in the Public Service, 1971

2. Resolution concerning the Future Work of the International Labour Organisation in the Field of Public Services, 1971

## VI. Reports and conclusions adopted by various technical meetings of the ILO

1. Conclusions Adopted by the Meeting of Experts on Conditions of Work and Service of Public Servants, 1963
2. Conclusions Adopted by the Meeting of Experts on the Relationship between Multinational Corporations and Social Policy, 1972

# Annex 2. Previous volumes in the Labour-Management Relations Series

No.
1. *The role of government in the field of labour-management relations: Canadian approach.* 1957. [E], [F], [S].
2. *Two examples of practical action to improve labour-management relations:*
   (1) *Peru*—July-August 1957. [E], [F], [S], and
   (2) *Bolivia*—October 1957. [E], [F], [S].
3. *Some aspects of labour-management relations in Asia.* 1958. [E].
4. *International standards and guiding principles, 1944–58.* 1958. (Amalgamated with Nos. 14, 24 and 34 and subsequently brought up to date as No. 44.)
5. *Workers' management and labour relations in Yugoslavia.* 1959. [E], [F].
6. *An account of an Asian Bipartite Study Tour on Labour-Management Relations to the United Kingdom and Federal Republic of Germany, 6 September-8 November 1958.* 1959. 205 pp. E, [S].
7. *The position and responsibilities of the personnel department inside undertakings.* 1960. 203 pp. [E], F, [S].
8. *Status and duties of workers' representatives.* 1960. 145 pp. E, F, S.
9. *Report to the Government of India on labour-management relations and some aspects of wages policy.* 1960. [E].
10. *Report on the visit of a joint team of experts on labour-management relations to Pakistan and Ceylon.* 1961. 89 pp. [E], S.
11. *Some aspects of labour-management relations in the American Region.* A summary of the discussions of the Inter-American Study Conference on Labour-Management Relations (Montevideo, 3–12 November 1960). 1961. E, S.
11(a). *Some aspects of labour-management relations in the American Region.* Report prepared by the International Labour Office for the Inter-American Study Conference on Labour-Management Relations (Montevideo, 3-12 November 1960). 1962. 176 pp. E, S.
12. *Personnel relations in a growing enterprise.* A case study of an Israeli undertaking. 1962. 107 pp. E, S.
13. *Consultation and co-operation between employers and workers at the level of the enterprise.* Outline of the regulations in force in 11 European countries. Report drawn up in collaboration with the OECD. 1962. 79 pp. E, F, [S].
14. *International standards and guiding principles, 1958–61.* 1962. (New, up-to-date editions published as Nos. 24, 34 and 44.)
15. *Prevention and settlement of industrial disputes in Asia.* Documents submitted to and report of an Asian Regional Seminar (Kuala Lumpur, 7–19 December 1961). 1962. 266 pp. [E], S.
16. *Government services for the improvement of labour-management relations and settlement of disputes in Asia.* An account of the work of the Labour-Management Relations Committee, Fifth Asian Regional Conference (Melbourne, 1962). 1963. 131 pp. [E], F.

[ . ] = out of print.

17. *Basic agreements and joint statements on labour-management relations.* 1963. 123 pp. (New, up-to-date edition published as No. 38.)
18. *Report to the Government of India on the organisation and development of a government personnel management advisory service.* 1963. 53 pp. E.
19. *Report to the Government of Turkey on the visit of a joint mission of experts on labour-management relations* (18 November–15 December 1962). 1963. 70 pp. E, F, S.
20. *The role of labour ministries in the improvement of labour-management relations in Latin America.* 1964. 43 pp. [E], S.
21. *Scope and methods of collective bargaining in the iron and steel industry.* Report submitted to and proceedings of the Seventh Session of the Iron and Steel Committee (Cardiff, 26 August–6 September 1963). 1964. 122 pp. E, F, S.
22. *Industrial relations in certain African countries.* Documentation and summary of proceedings of a Seminar on Industrial Relations (Abidjan, 15–26 October 1963). 1964. 361 pp. [E], F.
23. *Reports to the Government of Ceylon on labour-management relations training and on labour-management relations and personnel management at the Gal Ova Development Board.* 1964. 112 pp. E.
24. *International standards and guiding principles, 1944–64.* 1965. (New, up-to-date editions published as Nos. 34 and 44.)
25. *Certain aspects of labour-management relations within the undertaking.* Documents of a technical meeting (5–15 October 1964). 1965. 389 pp. E, F, S.
26. *Institutional aspects of labour-management relations inside undertakings in Asia.* Record of proceedings of and contributions submitted to an Asian Regional Seminar (Kandy, 19–30 April 1965). 1966. 223 pp. E.
27. *The role of employers' and workers' organisations in programming and planning in the metal trades.* Report submitted to and proceedings of the Eighth Session of the Metal Trades Committee (6–17 December 1965). 1967. 124 pp. E, F.
28. *Practical measures to promote good labour-management relations on plantations.* Report submitted to and proceedings of the Fifth Session of the Committee on Work on Plantations (2–13 May 1966). 1967. 186 pp. E, F.
29. *Methods of collective bargaining and settlement of disputes in rail transport.* Report submitted to and proceedings of the Eighth Session of the Inland Transport Committee (21 November–2 December 1966). 1967. 139 pp. E, F.
30. *Informe al Gobierno de la República del Perú sobre la mediación y conciliación de los conflictos colectivos de trabajo.* 1968. 55 pp. S.
31. *Labour-management relations in public industrial undertakings in Asia.* Report submitted to and proceedings of the 13th Session of the Asian Advisory Committee (Singapore, November–December 1966). 1968. [E].
32. *Rights of trade union representatives at the level of the undertaking.* Documents of a technical meeting (20–29 November 1967). 1969. 108 pp. E, F, S.
33. *Participation of workers in decisions within undertakings.* Documents of a technical meeting (20–29 November 1967). 1969. 165 pp. [E], F, [S].
34. *International standards and guiding principles, 1944–68.* 1969. 255 pp. [E], [F], [S]. (New, up-to-date edition published as No. 44.)
35. *Management development and personnel policies and practices in Asia.* An account of the work of the Management Development Committee, Sixth Asian Regional Conference (Tokyo, 1968). Second impression, 1975. 125 pp. E, F.
36. *The role of employers' and workers' organisations in programming and planning in the iron and steel industry.* 1970. 114 pp. E, F.

37. *Conciliation and arbitration of industrial disputes in English-speaking countries of Africa.* 1970. 208 pp. E.
38. *Basic agreements and joint statements on labour-management relations.* 1971. 248 pp. E, F, S.
39. *Role of employers' organisations in Asian countries.* Record of proceedings of and documents submitted to an Asian Round Table (Tokyo, December 1970). 1971. 344 pp. E.
40. *Industrial relations and personnel management in English-speaking Africa.* Record of proceedings of and documents submitted to a seminar (Dar es Salaam, October–November 1971). 1972. 204 pp. E.
41. *Freedom of association for workers' and employers' organisations and their role in social and economic development in Asia.* An account of the work of the Committee on Workers' and Employers' Organisations, Seventh Asian Regional Conference (Teheran, 1971). 1972. 86 pp. E, F.
42. *Role of employers' organisations in English-speaking African countries.* Record of proceedings of and documents submitted to an African Round Table (Addis Ababa, October 1972). 1973. iv + 170 pp. E.
43. *Labour relations in the Caribbean region.* 1974. 205 pp. E.
44. *International standards and guiding principles, 1944–73.* 1975. 369 pp. E, F, S.
45. *Social problems of contract, subcontract and casual labour in the petroleum industry.* Report submitted to and proceedings of the Eighth Session of the Petroleum committee (Geneva, 2–13 April 1973). 1974. 95 pp. E, F.
46. *Rôle des organisations d'employeurs dans les pays d'Afrique francophone.* Compte rendu d'une table ronde africaine (Abidjan, March–Arpil 1974). 1975. 150 pp. F.
47. *Employers' organisations and industrial relations in Asia.* Record of proceedings of and documents submitted to a Regional Technical Seminar on Industrial Relations for Employers' Organisations in Asian countries (Jakarta, November 1974). 1975. 254 pp. E.
48. *Workers' participation in decisions within undertakings.* Summary of discussions of a Symposium on Workers' Participation in Decisions within Undertakings, Oslo, 20–30 August 1974. 1976. 129 pp. E, F.
49. *The role of labour law in developing countries.* Record of proceedings of and documents submitted to a Round Table (Geneva, 10–14 September, and Selva di Fasano, Italy, 17–19 September 1974). 1975. 266 pp. E, F, S.
50. [Not published.]
51. *Papel de las organizaciones de empleadores en América Latina.* Documentos de una reunión técnica (Rio de Janeiro, 14–22 July 1975). 1976. 259 pp. S.
52. *Industrial relations in Asia.* Record of proceedings of and documents submitted to a Symposium (Manila, 26 August–6 September 1975). 1976. 284 pp. E.
53. *Role of employers' organisations in English-speaking Caribbean countries.* Record of proceedings of and documents submitted to a Caribbean Round Table (Montego Bay, Jamaica, 2–9 December 1975). 1977. iv + 151 pp. E.
54. *Role of employers' organisations in the Arab countries.* Record of the proceedings of a Round Table (Alexandria, 16–22 October 1976). Second impression, 1980. 58 pp. E, F. (A version in Arabic is available from the ILO Branch Office in Cairo.)
55. *Les salaires dans les pays d'Afrique francophone.* Compte rendu des travaux d'un séminaire regional OIT/DANIDA (Yaoundé, May 1977). 1978. 130 pp. F.
56. *Collective bargaining in industrialised countries: Recent trends and problems.* Vienna Symposium, 2–9 November 1977. 1978. ii + 113 pp. E, F.

57. *Wage determination in English-speaking Caribbean countries*. Record of proceedings of and documents submitted to an ILO/DANIDA Regional Seminar (Kingston, Jamaica, 1–7 March 1978). 1979. 121 pp. E.
58. *Wage determination in Asia and the Pacific: The views of employers' organisations*. Reports and documents submitted to an ILO/DANIDA Regional Seminar (Singapore, 8–12 October 1979). 1980. ii + 169 pp. E.
59. *Labour relations and development: Country studies on Japan, the Philippines, Singapore and Sri Lanka*. 1982. 153 pp. E.
60. *Labour-management relations in public enterprises in Africa*. 1983. 84 pp. E, F.
61. *Labour relations in Southern Africa*. Proceedings of and documents submitted to a Seminar (Gaborone, 2–4 December 1981). 1982. 58 pp. E.
62. *Conciliation services: Structures, functions and techniques*. 1983. iii + 141 pp. E.
63. *Selected basic agreements and joint declarations on labour-management relations*. 1983. 229 pp. E, S.
64. *Labour relations in Africa: English-speaking countries*. Proceedings of, and documents submitted to, a Symposium (Nairobi, 22–26 November 1982). 1983. 159 pp. E, F.
65. Beth Stevens: *Complementing the Welfare State: The developing of private pension, health insurance and other employee benefits in the United States*, Geneva, 1986, viii + 73 pp., price: 15 Swiss francs, ISBN 92-2-105673-2, A.
66. *Relaciones de trabajo en el Uruguay*. Informe de una misión de la Oficina Internacional del Trabajo, Ginebra, 1987, xiii + 192 págs., precio: 15 francos suizos, ISBN 92-2-306180-6, E.
67. *Assessing the impact of statutory minimum wages in developing countries: Four country studies*, Geneva, 1988, vii + 158 pp., price: 20 Swiss francs, ISBN 92-2-106204-X, A.
68. *Technological change, work organisation and pay: Lessons from Asia*, Geneva, 1988, price: 25 Swiss francs, ISBN 92-2-106324-0, A.
69. *Promotion of collective bargaining and protection of security of employment in English speaking African countries*, Geneva, 1988, price: 27.50 Swiss francs, ISBN 92-2-106355-0, A.
70. *European labour courts: Current issues*, Proceedings of the Second Meeting of European Labour Court Judges (Herzlia, Israel, December 1987), edited by Werner Blenk, Geneva 1989, vii + 85 pp., price: 15 Swiss francs, ISBN 92-2-106437-9, A.
71. *Current approaches to collective bargaining*. An ILO Symposium on Collective Bargaining in Industrialised Market Economy Countries (Geneva, 2–6 November 1987), Geneva, 1989, price: 22,50 Swiss francs, ISBN 92-2-106503-0, A.
72. *Problèmes actuels de la négociation collective*. Colloque de l'OIT sur la négociation collective dans les pays industrialisés à économie de marché (Genève, 2–6 nov. 1987), Genève, 1989, vii + 125 pp., prix: 17,50 francs suisses, ISBN 92-2-206412-7, F.
73. *Government wage policy formulation in developing countries: Seven country studies*, Geneva, 1989, viii + 128 pp., price: 17,50 Swiss francs, ISBN 92-2-106504-9, A.